Praise for

MW01202119

From navigating career crossroads to overcoming personal tragedies, the brave souls within these pages share their journeys of stepping into the unknown, facing their fears, and forging ahead by the light of the moon. Their candid accounts offer both inspiration and wisdom, reminding us that while the path may not be clear, there is always a way forward for those willing to take that courageous first step.

By the Light of the Moon is a profound exploration of the human spirit's capacity to persevere in the face of life's inevitable uncertainties. Let these stories be your guiding light, empowering you to embrace the unknown with courage and emerge from the darkness transformed and emboldened.

— ERIKA HULL, BESTSELLING AUTHOR OF ... *BUT THAT'S NOT ME AND NOTES FROM MOTHERLAND*

By the Light of the Moon is a cozy, deep, ritual connecting mystery and power, through true stories of life's wins and losses from a feminine perspective.

— TERESA CRUZ FOLEY, AUTHOR OF *MINDFULLY INCLUSIVE: CONNECTING SOCIAL EMOTIONAL LEARNING WITH DIVERSITY, EQUITY, AND INCLUSION SKILLS*

By the Light of the Moon is the perfect collection of stories to sit cuddled with your tea and get lost in, literally by the light of the moon. Without being cliche, every bit of it is real, raw, and relevant. Spanning topics from abandonment to zen, you're sure to find yourself somewhere in each author's story. I'd read it again and again!

— ASHLEY WIZE, BESTSELLING AUTHOR OF
NOTES FROM MOTHERLAND

Remarkable stories for anyone seeking encouragement in the face of fear or uncertainty. Brave and inspiring - highly recommended!

— MIMI RICH MA, MARRIAGE AND FAMILY
THERAPIST

By the light of the moon

AN
ANTHOLOGY

By the Light of the Moon

RED THREAD BOOKS

Red Thread Publishing LLC. 2024

Write to **info@redthreadbooks.com** if you are interested in publishing with Red Thread Publishing. Learn more about publications or foreign rights acquisitions of our catalog of books: www.redthreadbooks.com

This book compilation is initiated by Sierra Melcher, the founder of Red Thread Publishing. If you would like to be published as an author in our future book compilations such as this please visit www.redthreadbooks.com or email us at info@ redthreadbooks.com .

Paperback ISBN: 978-1-955683-60-9

Ebook ISBN: 979-8-89294-000-9

Cover Design: Red Thread Designs

The information and advice contained in this book are based upon the research and the personal and professional experiences of the authors. Some names and characteristics have been changed, some events have been compressed, and some dialogue has been recreated. Chapters reflect the authors' present recollections of experiences over time. The opinions herein are of each individual contributor. All writings are the property of individual contributors.

The publisher and authors are not responsible for any adverse effects or consequences resulting from the use of any of the suggestions, preparations, or procedures discussed in this book.

Dedication

Just because you cannot see a path does not mean there is not a way forward. To those who are momentarily lost.

Epigraph

"Feeling lost doesn't mean you are lost."

— SIERRA MELCHER

Contents

Publisher's Note

Dear Reader,

Welcome to *By the Light of the Moon*. Before embarking on this journey through the heartfelt stories within these pages, we wish to offer a prelude regarding the sensitive topics that are delicately explored.

This anthology is a tapestry of personal narratives, each woven with authenticity and vulnerability. Within these stories, you will find candid discussions about being human.

Additionally, we want to acknowledge that some stories within this anthology contain sensitive topics. We understand that these topics can be triggering for some readers, and we advise discretion while reading.

We encourage you to approach these stories with an open heart and mind, knowing that each author's journey is a testament to the power of resilience, love, and the human spirit.

Thank you for joining us on this poignant exploration of human-hood from the female lense. May these stories resonate with you as deeply as they have with us.

May it ripple,
Red Thread Publishing

Introduction

by Sierra Melcher

If you've ever walked in the woods at night you know the feeling; maybe there is a path. Maybe you're on it but it's hard to tell. In the daylight we try to stay on the path of the safe, the known. Walking in the woods by moonlight there's no *one* sure way. There are countless ways forward to find your way.

Life can be much more uncertain.

It can be scary. Terrifying. When the sun shines, we want to stay on the known road. But there are times in life where there is not one clear or safe path.

In any case, we all must walk forward. Navigating the unknown by the light of the moon, where every step is a little bit of a risk, shows us what we're capable of. Not only does stepping into the unknown lead us to a different destination but we are also changed by the process, forged in that uncertainty, strengthened by facing those fears and choosing to step forward anyway.

We have all walked by the light of the moon, we've all doubted ourselves in that space of uncertainty. Some of us lucky enough to find a way forward have shared our stories here. Maybe you have one or several; maybe you have stayed still waiting for the sun to rise.

But there is always a way forward for those brave enough to walk it. May the stories shared here impart some of their strength and their wisdom to you. May the voices echo in your heart bringing resilience to you and your journey and the next time you find yourself alone in the dark, lost in the woods, let some of these stories be the light.

Chapter One

SHADOWS OF THE NIGHT

FRANCES D. TREJO-LAY

H ave you ever heard the sound of a heart breaking? I have.

"Fraaannnnnnnces!"

Rick cries out in anguish. A wail of pure sorrow. Something bad is happening.

I stumble out of bed and make my way to the bedroom door, to the top of the stairs, blinking, barely awake.

It is around noon, on the last Sunday in May 2021.

I sleep in because I was up until 3 AM watching an anime with our 20-year-old son. During the Pandemic, my son and I do that a lot. In fact, I had a weird sleep pattern during COVID-19 lockdown. Going to bed around 2 or 3 AM and waking around noon.

Stumbling down the stairs, I see the aqua curtain billowing through the open sliding glass door. I see Rick in his orange t-shirt and boxers pacing nervously between the pool and the glass doors.

I hear Rick choking back sobs as he cries:

"Peppy...he fell... in the.... pool! And... He died!"

Rick is inconsolable. This man rarely cries.

I pick up Peppy's little body from the edge of the pool. I'm weeping. I hold my 5-pound chihuahua in my arms— not caring that my nightgown is getting wet. Yes, Peppy is gone, his body is stiff–there is no saving him. I put him back down.

I hug Rick and we cry.

*Still choking back tears, I wrap up my sweet little "chi" in a towel. I put his body in the blue pet taxi we **used to** carry our little dogs to the vet. It feels especially painful to lose Peppy today because Shelby, our 8-pound chi-weenie mix died the previous May.*

Our home feels instantly empty after Peppy dies. We no longer have dogs in our home. A gaping hole opens where cuddles, laughs and unconditional love flowed for 15 years.

Later, I witness Rick's heart actually break.... Four days later he has a heart attack.

I won't share the story of Rick's heart attack– it's too traumatic. Know that he is alive and well today, managing his heart health with a vegan diet and regular exercise. He never feels cardiac pains and remembers only little flashes of that day.

The story I will share with you is how the Universe got me through this crisis. I will share how this life-changing event impacted me and helped me step into accepting parts of myself I was having trouble accepting.

We all have parts of ourselves we do not like: our flaws, limiting beliefs and patterns of negative behavior, our "dark side." "Shadow Work," shines a light on these flaws and what lessons we can learn from them. By the light of the moon, we can learn to embrace all parts of ourselves: the light *and the dark.*

I have a recurring negative pattern that kicks in **hard** in times of crisis. In a crisis, it's as if the problem is tearing a hole in the beautiful fabric of my life and it must be "fixed" immediately. I go into this driving, obsessive frenzy of "doing/fixing." I do not take breaks, eat, rest nor sleep until my world is whole again. No matter how much my body aches or how bad I feel, the adrenaline keeps me going. This dark pattern has been a part of me for decades because it gives me results; I earn A's and praise for what gets accomplished in this vortex of deprivation and emotional upheaval. *But at what cost?*

In early 2019, I started feeling excruciating pain all over my body, all day, every day, for months. I am taking nerve blockers around the clock to function. I rest a lot and do minimal housework. I barely exercise and stand up for only short periods. I give up crochet and knitting so I can still cook. I'm terrified that this unbearable pain is some horrible lifelong disease. Deep down some part of me wonders if I'm being punished for something I have done. I don't want to be in this much pain every day.

I don't get a diagnosis despite a year of taking lab tests and seeing specialists. By the time a rheumatologist tells me she has no idea what is wrong with me, it's 2020 and we are deep into the Covid Lockdown. It's extremely difficult to follow up on non-emergency health care. Frustrated, I look for answers elsewhere. *What if this is psychological?*

My story "Circles" in *Planting the Seed,* (2023) details how I found my way to Women's Circles. In weekly Circle, I learn and practice **deep listening** and start hearing my own intuition more and more clearly.

In Women's Circles, I learn the importance of doing things for **both my body and soul**. To help my body I stretch, move, and take rest breaks. For my soul, I return to the joy and pleasure of exploring, playing, and admiring nature and beauty. More importantly, I cultivate my relationship with the Divine.

Spirituality is such a huge part of my upbringing. God and I were really close in the past. My connection to the Divine meant the world to me during my youth. *What happened?*

Time for some shadow work.

I journal about my early bond with God as a little girl. The bond is forged from the Bible stories I hear and the little movies I see in my mind's eye as I listen. I love these stories and the people in them. God, Jesus, the Holy Spirit, Mother Mary, Noah, the Apostles, and St. Francis of Assisi are some of my favorite people. Somehow, I understand that they are not here on this Earth "in the flesh" but that they exist in some other place and help us whenever we ask.

This bond deepens in my teens. I am involved in Catholic Youth Leadership from the ages of 14-18, and I'm at Church every Sunday singing at Mass. I attend Catholic Youth rallies; I hear Mother Teresa and Pope John Paul II speak. God sends me little movies–visions–when I pray in Prayer Group. *Whoa!* God has been communicating with me like this my entire childhood! I feel so free, so "seen" and "taken care of" by God. *So why am I here now at almost 50, in so much pain and feeling so lost?*

More shadow work.

I share in Women's Circle and I keep journaling. I recall that in my twenties, I moved from my hometown to UC Santa Barbara's off-campus housing. I lose my close-knit spiritual community and don't bond with the local Catholic Church. I gradually pull away from the Divine. *Yikes!* It's been 27 years since I have nurtured myself and a connection to Source.

Women's Circle teaches me ways to connect with Source through the Divine Feminine. I explore a wide array of gentle spiritual practices and intuitive tools. I love the way drawing Oracle Cards "tells me" what I need to hear. They feel like my visions but in beautiful static pictures. I study the cycles of nature, the stars, planets, seasons, and especially the moon. I notice their influence on my energy. I explore Reiki and other ways of healing and relieving stress. I listen to solfeggio healing music and meditate.

I notice the Divine Feminine rituals and practices I adopt, expanding my intuition. When I close my eyes to meditate, I still see little movies in my mind's eye and now the visions are enhanced. I hear keywords and phrases, I have 'knowings' and I sense emotions. All of these intuitive whispers are messages from the Divine. The messages are often affirmed by *synchronicities*: images, objects, or symbols repeated in other spaces or by people with no possible connection to the original message. It's the Universe reassuring us we are on the right track.

The shadow work brings me back to one of my heart's greatest desires—a connection to The All. And surprise, surprise: the more I put myself first, by taking care of my body and soul every day, the less and less my body aches.

~

I do not doubt that the Universe has my back, but when Rick had a heart attack on June 3rd, I still reacted like a normal human being facing a crisis. My negative behavior patterns got triggered.

My "doing/fixing" pattern is very helpful in an emergency. On the day, I jump into action and call the paramedics. Rick gets evaluated and whisked away via helicopter to UCSD's Cardiac Cath Lab for an emergency stent procedure.

~

When we come home the "doing/fixing" behavior pattern is already wearing me out. I discovered two days later, I'm also having PTSD symptoms.

First, I can't fall asleep, nor stay asleep. I wake up several times a night and listen intently for Rick's breathing. Sometimes I stare at his shadow, making sure I see it rise and fall with every breath. Sometimes I feel for it, but stop because it startles him awake.

The second symptom is an extremely sensitive startle reflex. Surprising someone in our house is easy to do: our open floor plan creates very strange acoustics. My son managed to scare me twice because I didn't hear him coming. I jump as if touching a live electrical wire. I sweat profusely and my heart pounds hard–for 10-20 minutes. This is **way** too big of a reaction for such a little scare.

The third symptom is not being able to turn off my brain. The first ten days we were home, I was overwhelmed and obsessing about how to prevent another heart attack. I throw myself into "doing/fixing." As the family cook, it's a huge responsibility to learn new ways of cooking without adding oil, fat, and salt. The worst part is arguing with Rick about his unsafe activity choices.

I clearly hear the surgeon state that Rick needs to take it easy, slowly returning to regular exercise. Rick insists he can return to normal activities when he "feels better." This is an unreliable measure of wellness in Rick's case because he never feels cardiac pain. He is so gung-ho to return to his crazy workout competitions, *I want to throttle him!* I don't want to be fighting with Rick. Yet, I feel him pushing for the old 'normal,' not understanding that he has a *new normal.* I am frustrated by Rick's denial. There is severe damage to his heart: the part that doesn't get oxygen *dies* and turns into scar tissue. *The remaining healthy heart has to work that much harder* to pump blood through the body. Rick's body needs time to get used to the new workload. He needs to remember that he still has a vein that is 70% blocked and is scheduled for a second surgery in a month.

For 10 days, I have been looking up articles about post-stent surgery care; getting friends and family to convince Rick to slow down; looking up recipes; cooking, and debating with Rick. When I find him sneaking in an adrenaline-pumping Virtual Reality game, I chew him out. I feel like I have to watch him like a hawk. This constant "doing/fixing" is exhausting and the PTSD shows no signs of going away.

Then one day, I remember hearing "... the energy with which you approach a task/problem is just as important as the action taken." This is a Divine nudge. Take a break, and dance a little because it releases tension and brings me joy. I connect to Source and find the words I need.

The next time we are in the car alone together I say, "Rick, I need you to understand something really important. I don't want to be nagging you. Clearly, one set of behaviors and habits will lead to us losing you. Following another set of behaviors will have you live longer. Your son and I need you to choose the behaviors that will have you in our lives the longest."

It sinks in. Rick promises to only go on light walks for exercise between now and next month's stent surgery.

Welcome to my "dark side," in all its *glory.* It's soul-sucking. The obsessing fuels the PTSD and the PTSD won't let me release tension. It all loops together, making me feel worse.

I lay in bed, awake for the tenth night in a row. Rick sleeps peacefully. I searched YouTube for the solfeggio healing music I **used to** fall asleep to.

I play one for an hour and don't fall asleep. I play a different one for thirty minutes–staring into the darkness of my bedroom. The damn breaks. I start crying so hard my shoulders are shaking.

I feel so defeated. I seem to have zero control over my own body. I feel tears fall from the corners of my eyes into my hair as I lay there. I desperately beg, "Please God, take this away. I just can't anymore." I sob for a long while.

The tears gradually slow down and I take deep breaths.

Again, I flip through YouTube. Now I find a "Solfeggio Music for Healing PTSD" video. I wipe my eyes with the bed sheet, snuggle up into my pillows, and close my eyes. Immediately I start visioning.

I see darkness all around... a great void. As the music plays. I see pops of rainbow colors light up and go out. It's a sign from the Universe—I love rainbows! Rainbows are my favorite "color." Rainbows show up a lot in my visions. I also remember that it is "a symbol of God's promise..." Noah sees one in the sky after the Great Flood.

The void gets brighter. The sun is slowly rising. Pops of rainbow color reveal wispy-thin white clouds in the sky. I hear an angel Chorus singing a crescendo. I'm lying on my side and feel happy tears, fall across my nose, to my temple, and onto the pillow. Hearing Angels sing, is a perfect synchronicity. The first prayer I ever learn is a prayer to my guardian angel when I am three. My little girl faith warms and soothes my heart. I am powerfully connecting to angels and God again. The sky is bright blue now, with fluffy white clouds lazily drifting by. I notice when the angelic chorus repeats, it lights up the clouds in rainbow lights.

I feel a presence to my right. We are both flying through the clouds together! I see my dog Shelby who died a year ago, flying with these big white wings. Communicating mind to mind I say, "Shelby?" Then midflight, Shelby rolls a quarter turn in place, exposing her pink belly to me and holding her paws close to her chest. She holds the pose for a few seconds.

This is definitely my Shelby! It's her "show me the belly" pose when she wants tummy rubs. She gracefully continues the turn, does a fancy aerial flip, and returns to my right.

*I feel another presence to my left. It's Peppy awkwardly flying next to me. I have this **knowing** that Peppy needs more practice because he only started flying two weeks ago! I watch him concentrate. Shelby can do tricks because she has lived longer with her wings. Time flows differently where they are. One year for us is much more time where they are.*

Shelby "speaks" to my mind, "Mommy, we're okay. You are okay. Everything is going to be okay." followed by the crescendo of the angelic chorus. I wipe away more happy tears.

I release ALL the tension. I am filled with so much gratitude. It's such an unexpected joy to see my beloved pups thriving. The Divine message they deliver puts me at ease. A huge weight has been lifted and my neck and shoulders finally unclench. I can breathe and my mind stops racing.

After this vision, I feel different. I no longer jump sky-high when startled. My husband takes it easy. I am confident "everything will be okay." Our new normal isn't scary anymore and is becoming routine— our "normal."

~

I hope that by witnessing my shadow work, you can see that it gives me a new perspective on why I react the way I do. It also helps me catch the "dark" habit as it's happening, so I can choose something different. The magic of this work is that "dark" habits lead to growth and change. Shadow work isn't so scary, right? Maybe next time you are frustrated by behaviors you see yourself doing repeatedly and they hurt you, you will give shadow work a try. What you learn may surprise you!

My shadow work gave me an additional gift; I no longer fear telling people I see visions. It is the magical way Source and I communicate. The Divine made it possible for Peppy and Shelby to visit me, in some real and amazing way. I don't sweat wondering *how* it happens. I used to worry that people would call me a "crazy lady into 'woo-woo' shit." Now, I don't really care because it heals and empowers me.

Sharing this vision with others keeps strengthening my bond with Source and God keeps expanding my intuitive gifts. I see visions and "hear" messages that teach me about my humanity and my divinity.

The morning after my vision, I told Rick about it. He draws comfort from knowing that our dogs are happily flying around a kind of heaven.

Using my dark habits and "freakouts" as teachable moments, Source is teaching me to accept ALL of myself. I am on this planet at this time by Grace. *I know in the cockles of my soul, I am loved and cherished by Spirit. AND The Universe has given me intuitive gifts to share with the world.*

By the light of the moon, I accept that God loves me EXACTLY as I am.

I accept myself as I am.

About the Author
Frances D. Trejo-Lay

Frances (Frankie) Trejo-Lay is a Women's Circle Facilitator. She helps women reconnect to their own intuition. By teaching **deep listening** in the sacred space of Women's Circle, women "hear" their own inner voice with clarity and rediscover the joy of manifesting their heart's deepest desires.

She is also an Energy worker offering Distance Reiki/Energy work to friends and family. She looks forward to offering intuitive and energy work to clients in the near future. Frankie is a published author with Red Thread Publishing, contributing to four anthologies: Sanctuary (2022), Planting the Seed (2023), By the Light of the Moon (2024) and Motherland (2024).

Frankie speaks Spanglish at home with her husband and adult son in the Southern California Desert. They want a dog soon. Please subscribe for links to: register for the next Community Women's Circle and for new offerings.

linktr.ee/frances_trejo_lay_SacredSpace

Chapter Two

THE FIRST AND LAST LIES
BRANDEE MELCHER

MY BODY KNEW.

I t was later than he usually came home from the driving range, his new "me time" activity since starting his sobriety journey almost two years ago. I thought it was odd how late it was, but didn't really give it much thought - other than I didn't want to go to bed without saying good night so I stayed up. 10:00 pm came and he still wasn't home, so I began my nightly routine. There was also something tugging at me...telling me to stay up...telling me there was something I needed to see. I quieted the voice in my head and as I was passing through the kitchen, on the way to the bedroom, I could hear him fumbling with his keys in the lock of the front door while managing the golf bag. He was mumbling under his breath as he was attempting to quietly unlock the door. I headed towards the door and stopped - my body felt prickly all over, much like how I imagined a cactus might feel. It was as if billions of tiny needles had just pushed through my skin all over my body.

This is a weird sensation.

Before I could make it to the door and unlock it, he was in and was more animated than usual and I instantly knew why my body went into battle mode and the voice told me to stay awake... **Tim had been drinking.**

As I stood in the kitchen listening to him ecstatically recount his evening out, I hoped I was wrong. I honestly didn't even know if the driving range sold alcoholic beverages - naive, I know - so I asked. He quickly rattled off what he *thought* they sold. Next, I asked about his excited and overly animated behavior. He brushed it off stating he had a really great time and his swings were great and the balls landed where he wanted them to go. I knew it was more than that, so I asked "Have you been drinking?" It's a question I have never asked in the past year since he started going to the driving range because as his former bartender, I *know* when he's been drinking.

Tim looked at me, slightly shocked that I had asked and stammered through a response "...No. NO! I just had a really great time. I hit the ball perfectly, it did what I wanted. It was a great night."

He lied. He lied with little hesitation and I knew - did he know I knew? He intentionally lied. He's never lied to me in the past two years we've been on this sobriety journey - hell, I don't believe he's ever intentionally lied to me in our 14-year relationship. It's no secret in all of my relationships I value honesty & integrity above all and abhor lying due to my upbringing. I tell myself I'm wrong and remind myself it's almost 11:00 and 5:30 comes too early, so I hesitantly prepare for bed. Tim joins shortly after and we go to sleep.

Two weeks go by and he goes to the driving range again.

Not once during these two weeks did I mention his lying. Not once did I bring up my suspicions. I tell myself since this was the only time in two years that he's slipped, then *maybe* I could overlook it. Since this is the first lie in 14 years, then *maybe* it will be the last. I'm lying to myself. I know I am and yet, I'm still questioning what I know to be true.

It's getting late and my body tenses in anticipation of him coming home full of alcohol and lies. He finally comes home and I **know** he's been drinking. I ask and again he lies.

This time we go to bed at about the same time and in the safety and comfort of the darkened bedroom I gently nudge. Staring up at the ceiling, speaking slowly and deliberately, I lay the gauntlet.

"I know you've been drinking. I don't know why you lied to me but I know you've been drinking and I know you lied the last time...I know you and I know how you are when you drink. You need to get help. I can't continue to live like this and I told you last time what would happen if you drank."

Silence...then gentle sobs as Tim replies "...I'm so sorry. I don't know why I lied. I guess it was shame and thinking I could hide it."

We cry, hold each other as we go off to sleep and begin the cycle again. Or so I thought. I didn't realize that this was the beginning of the end. This was the beginning of me holding my boundaries with the one person I always bent to.

Fourteen years together, eleven years of marriage, two amazing children, four cats, two dogs, a house and a decent career - life was good. It wasn't anything exceptional and it was good and steady - typical suburbia. Not exactly the life I had imagined when we married and it was still a very good life.

After several years of arguments, individual and couples therapy and several weeks of intensive outpatient rehab in 2019, I thought we were finally on the other side. I thought we were finally moving towards the future we'd been discussing & planning. I thought the girls and I were finally enough. The cracks in the foundation we had built and repaired in 2019 and 2020 began to grow and this time, in February 2021, there was not a way to repair them.

Neither one of us knew it at the time that we were at the beginning of the end. I felt like we were back at the beginning of a cycle I was tired of repeating. A cycle I had participated in for several years. A cycle I thought we had finally ended in 2020. A cycle I could blindly walk through because we'd been here so many times before. A cycle that was like a well-worn path through the woods, and to step off of it would result in an immediate stumble so you stay on the path...even if you don't like the destination.

In the moment, I didn't know what to do. I had educated myself on alcoholism or as some call it, alcohol use disorder, to the point that I was sick and past the point of continued learning. Alcoholism and co-dependent education filled my downtime. I knew it wasn't my job to fix him and I couldn't cure his alcoholism and yet, I wanted, **needed**, answers. I needed it to stop. I wanted my marriage and yet...I didn't want this life anymore. I didn't want a life where I had to wonder each time I left the house if I would be returning home to a drunk spouse. I didn't want a life wondering if my children were being properly cared for because their father was intoxicated. I didn't want a life where I felt like an option.

I grew up feeling like an option to my parents. Even though they felt forced to have me, I knew I was never their number one priority. This partnership, this marriage, this *was* an option. An option he asked for and I said *yes* to, so we chose each other...and yet, I was being placed second to a substance.

Right after our youngest turned one in December of 2018, I told him I couldn't do this again. I had told him that if he drank like this again the marriage was over. Threatening to end the marriage was an ultimatum. I had hoped it was a way to control our future and force him to choose me. To choose the family. To choose us. I had hoped it was a way to stop the drinking and this loop we were frequently in. Now I had a choice. I could back down like I had all the years prior or this time I could stand by what I said, even if I didn't know if that's what I really wanted.

I was in disbelief. I simply couldn't believe we were here again. That I was here again.

Wasn't I worth it? Weren't our children worth it? Isn't our future worth it? Isn't our marriage worth it?

I had to know why he did it. I had to know why he was willing and thought he was able to pay the bill with our marriage. When the bartender handed him the bill and said your total is "$6," Tim handed him his card and offered up the marriage as a tip.

Against my better judgment, I asked. I needed an answer, even if I knew it was going to break me.

I told him I didn't expect an answer immediately, that he could take his time but I needed to know how he made that decision, knowing that it could break the family. I explained how I struggled to justify buying myself the skincare I love because of the potential *financial* implications to the family so I needed to know how he could make such a selfish decision that would impact the structure of the family.

He came back within 24 hours. "Because I wanted to. Because I wanted a drink like everyone else. Because it's what **I** wanted" he said with conviction and without shame or guilt.

In that moment, my soul broke. It was acute and so painful that I quickly scanned my body to ensure I didn't somehow just break a bone. We were suddenly two people moving on separate paths toward different futures; we just didn't know it.

I'm not sure what hurt more - his complete disregard for us or the fact he had intentionally lied for the first time in our marriage.

I was still processing the events from the past month, the lie and his eventual brutal honesty. Sure, there had been unintentional betrayals when I would come home and find him drunk after he said he wasn't doing that anymore. His decision to lie was different. He never intended to get passed out drunk; it just happened as he poured one too many heavy drinks. It was a by-product of his actions - not a conscious decision. I'd like to believe that as he poured his beverages, he never thought about how he was lying to me and himself. That he didn't precisely choose to get drunk, knowing it was going to cause problems. It just happened because he wasn't aware of his limits.

Even still, I was trying. I was following all of the people in recovery I could find on social media, I was suggesting sober people for him to follow, I was reading books and articles, I was grasping for ANYONE who could provide guidance and tell me this would work. I wanted someone, anyone, to tell me that what I knew to be true in my gut was wrong. I didn't want to accept the fact that I was slowly letting go. That maybe...I had been letting go. I didn't want to accept the fact I wanted a divorce. I didn't want to accept the fact that my love had changed. I wanted to continue to deny what my body was telling me. I had spent so many years telling my body to be quiet and rationalizing that I just wanted those things to keep being true because it was easier. It was easier to keep living this life and ignoring myself.

After the break, my body could no longer be quiet. She began speaking up more clearly, firmly and lovingly. There was wisdom she had been attempting to share for years; now, the dam had broken, and I could no longer keep her quiet. We argued. I'd rationalize with her. I'd bargain with her. I'd counter her knowing with past actions and history; she'd remind me of what I had pushed aside in those moments. She was here to hold me as I began to accept what my body had known for so long. My body had been patiently waiting all these years for me to finally listen.

To admit all of that would have meant it was over, truly over and I didn't know how to reconcile that fact within. Others saw it. They would comment how I was more upset about my job than the state of my marriage. They would ask, am I sure I still want to try? They would try to guide me to the answer we all knew was there and yet I couldn't say out loud. Because to say it out loud would mean that it was now alive and not a quiet secret I could conceal. To give breath to the desire for divorce, I wasn't ready to admit it to myself or anyone else. It would create an opportunity for someone else, and myself, to witness my pain and make it real.

I remember reading Glennon Doyle's *Love Warrior* and equating my husband's alcoholic lying to infidelity and thinking *if Glennon could find a way, then maybe so could I*. Alcoholism and infidelity are not the exact same - one is rooted in disease, the other in choices; however both alcoholics and adulterers carry the same traits: lying, betrayal, bargaining, codependency and ultimately hurt - internally and externally. In my desperation, it made sense. The only flaw in my plan is that Glennon did find her way and it still led to divorce.

There was no avoiding it.

As my personal therapist had said, "The train has left the station and you are on your way. You can't see the destination right now and you'll know it when you get there." I knew it. I had reached my destination and yet I blew past the stop in the hope that the next stop was where I truly belonged, where everyone could be happy and I could be content enough.

I mainly wondered how many more times I'd be in this cycle before I finally ended the marriage...because that was the only answer, it was only a matter of time.

~

The marriage ended officially on May 18, 2023. Over a year past our initial separation and over two years since the last relapse. To come to the decision to divorce, especially with two small children to consider, was not an easy path and it was the correct one for me and all people involved. I had to slowly bring to light the truths I had been ignoring. The path to separation and ultimately divorce was slowly revealed over time, much like the phases of the moon. I had to slowly illuminate the parts of me I had been ignoring.

I had to learn to acknowledge my codependence, stop the mental gymnastics, set clear boundaries and really dig into the lesser-known parts of my being without judgment and with gentle compassion. Coming to terms with being married to a high-functioning alcoholic was a journey that took years to admit. It took almost as long to realize that I couldn't cure his disease, no matter how hard I tried. In my book *The Break: Rediscovering Our Inner Knowing*, I explore how accepting this truth and finally honoring the wisdom of my body led to ending a relationship that fulfilled the status quo while leaving me empty.

It takes courage to bring the darker parts of you to the light and accept your whole self. I had to come to terms with my contribution to the alcoholic cycle. I had to accept my codependent traits and then learn how to break those habits. I couldn't do it all at once. It had to be addressed in progressive phases. I came to realize I was worthy in all the phases of this rediscovery of myself - even on the nights I melted into the corner of my kitchen crying because I felt so hollow and couldn't figure out how I'd gotten to this moment. That dark part of me that I didn't show to the light was still just as worthy, as the smiles and laughter I showed to the world once I returned to myself.

Everything moves through phases, including yourself. When things seem as dark as a new moon night and there is barely any light to find your way, know that the light is coming. Small shifts, turns and acknowledgements of your inner knowing will bring you back towards the light. Just like the moon is always there in the sky, not always visible, your inner knowing is always there waiting for you, even when it's a little quiet.

About the Author
Brandee Melcher

Brandee Melcher is an author and mother who is continually working to undo the lessons she was taught growing up that no longer serve her or her children. She is teaching her daughters and other women in her circle to pay attention to their inner knowing by taking the time to focus inward and quiet the outside world with tips found in her weekly newsletter.

Brandee lives just outside of Raleigh, North Carolina in her house that is in a constant state of improvement—much like herself. In between raising her two daughters and the corporate job, she spends most of her time reading, working in her garden, going for jogs, and visiting lighthouses in all shapes and sizes.

linktr.ee/brandeemelcher807

Chapter Three

25 LINES THAT CAN BE IN A LOVE LETTER OR SUICIDE NOTE

HANNAH TZEITEL STOKES

1. Time's up. Do we define what our home is? Or do we get thrust into convoluted ideas of safety that become intertwined with the sweet nothing on your lips? You make love to a version of yourself with cigarette burns lacing up your arms.
2. I can still imagine the light in my eyes when my grandmother was stroking the golden hair of an untouched 5-year-old. You saw her beyond the confinements of us, beyond the ashtray I became.
3. How do we forgive ourselves for the things we can't become in a world that pushes us to every limit imaginable?
4. I broke myself trying to be the idealized version of romance that you can't live without.
5. The bruises on the bearings of my bones mean nothing compared to what I saw that night in you. It was the first time I saw sightings of untoward creatures crawling up the whites of your eyes. Creatures that visit me every night in terrors that makes no sense.
6. I miss my soul, when cigarettes were candy and love was still a fantasy. When Vyvanse was ibuprofen and vodka shots were just Shirley temples. When sex was something special

and there weren't any tits to commodify. I wish I could be heartbroken by an insignificant love, but it gets clouded by the man who used to beat me. Innocence is something only certain kids get to know for a finite amount of time.

7. Your song doesn't exist anymore. You walk into your bathroom to see toilet paper stacked in an astronomical tower of fuckery and you can't remember how or why. "Rose-colored glasses" turn into broken spectacles of a love that's meaning I keep forgetting.

8. These constructs of thought that have facilitated notions of selling my body for a good time turn into the nothing you now are.

9. I can still see the lines on your wrist that morph into little slices of heaven shooting up our noses.

10. Mariposa Street. The fight you have with yourself every day. Just walk in and let the water fill your lungs like the way he stole all the life from you 5 years ago. But you refuse because you've already been there for so fucking long. You refuse to let the idea they created overcome your senses, yet they somehow do.

11. I know you liked me better at eighteen. Sex, drugs, money all in that order; it makes you miss all your dead friends. You see figures in the corner of your eye praying that you've gone back in time to when they still had air in their lungs.

12. I'm lying because I'm scared of the truth. Scared that I can't live with the broken dreams of a 15-year-old. Scared of witnessing pictures in the reflections of teardrops that roll down my porcelain skin.

13. Coffee mixed with notions of suicide. Every morning, you're overcome with the bittersweetness that was us. I wanted to die then too. Death. The ever-ending moment in which we fall back into swaths of soil that have been waiting for our precious kiss.

14. Stop pretending it's a history I can escape. I learned that no one can alter my heart after what you stole from me.

15. I can see flashbacks in the smoke of a soul Before him. Before he engulfed my flame with war-torn memories of a life I shouldn't know.

16. I wish I could remember what ennui feels like—the repetitive nature of two souls intertwining to lose their own breath in each other's eyes.

17. Starting riots in your head with people who never knew you and never will.

18. The war. Battlefields covered in the carnage of slutty versions of yourself. They're all on their knees begging for a pistol.

19. Pain. It involves becoming obsessed with a light that sparks his own flame. It's seeing your first love drown himself in lies of a past life. It's letting a man wrap his hand so tight around your neck you forget who you are. It's watching the clouds pass as you sit in the same spot he forced his cock down your throat.

20. The split. The versions of myself that have been created in order to breathe fresh air. Putting myself in unknown positions to feel a sliver of anything. Random dicks and little white lines of bliss don't work anymore.

21. Case numbers. A night that will follow me for the rest of my days, all reduced down to a set of letters and numbers.

22. The old me. A Barbie manufactured by men with holes in their eyes. Remembering the growth.

23. Forgiving. Learning to see through every horrid action this life has thrown toward you. Forgiving yourself and those you love for the heartbreaks of this life.

24. Watching the smiles of unbroken children as they begin again.

25. Time's not up. The flowers still bloom every year on my birthday.

About the Author

Hannah Tzeitel Stokes

Hannah Tzeitel Stokes has been writing her entire life. She is a student at the University of Colorado Denver studying Political Science and Sociology with an emphasis in Gender Relations. She is passionate about challenging conventional societal norms and emphasizes her ability to talk about challenging subjects. She strives to continue to help people find their voice, in whatever way that may be. linktr.ee/hantstokes

Chapter Four

COUNTLESS UNKNOWN GIFTS AWAIT

SIERRA MELCHER

Reminder:

I have it in me to do it again

"I came to Colombia so you could break up with me to my face."

People often ask me how I came to live in Colombia and why I've been here for the last 14 years. It's a long story. But I'll keep it simple.

It was the first time I'd ever fallen in love. It was the first time I let myself open, be seen, and care for another. I was 28 years old.

I jumped into this experience, wholeheartedly and with abandon. So it follows that the breakup required all of me as well. I was in uncharted territory from day one.

I had lost the first job I ever loved, teaching at a high school in San Francisco, due to a school closure. That same summer, reeling from the transition in my career, I realized that I had lived a closed-off life and I committed to opening my heart, and my mind. Periodically throughout my life, I have jumped in with both feet, to that thing which most scared me, challenged me, and offered something more in this chapter of my life. Unemployed, I committed to recuperating and recommitted to living my life fully.

With the time spread out in front of me, I knew I needed to learn to trust people in general. In 2006 I discovered *Couchsurfing*. Way before Airbnb, *Couchsurfing* was built on a philosophy of connecting people from around the world not based on an economic gain, but with the intention of building community and creating cross-cultural bonds. It was the coolest thing I'd ever seen. So I opened my studio apartment on Golden Gate Park in San Francisco to guests.

Over one hundred people from 42 countries came to stay with me. There was no money exchanged. It's been one of the greatest experiments of my life. For the next few years in San Francisco, then later in Shanghai, and eventually in Colombia, I hosted travelers, guests, and strangers. I have been featured in the media in several countries and I solo traveled on a shoestring budget several times through Europe, crashing with fellow *Couchsurfers*, (before the community got sold and turned into a bastardized version of itself, more like a hookup app than its original intention.)

The experiment itself changed me. I met best friends and people that irrevocably changed the trajectory of my life.

He walked right into my house, into my life and into my heart, a young Colombian guy named John. Like so many ignorant, ill-informed people I was apprehensive and honestly a bit nervous to welcome two Colombian guys into my house. But he and his friend had commented on the pictures of my book collection and as literature students seemed harmless.

For three days, he stayed in my house with his friend. We enjoyed the Bluegrass Festival, Indian food, and cheap beer. During the day I was drafting the first manuscript I would never publish while they wandered the city. At night, we discussed life: bad reggaeton (Colombian music), culture, and our shared love of literature. But there was zero attraction. The third night, however, while sitting and talking something shifted.

Sitting near each other in my bay window overlooking Golden Gate Park, engaged in a debate about something. Then he got up and sat on the couch on the other side of the room. I was struck by the most intense sensation; *he is too far away,* I thought. I got up. I sat down next to him and my knee gently brushed his and that was it. From that moment onward, we knew we were together.

He and his friend had intended to stay only three days, but they stayed 30. We took a road trip down the coast of California: a pilgrimage to a graveyard of some favorite rocker of theirs in Hollywood, and even to Las Vegas.

In the very last moment before his visa expired, we said goodbye. He had to leave the country. I had spent a month falling in love with a total stranger. I didn't have to work. Head over heels, then he was gone. We didn't know if he could ever come back.

Cities surround us with so much ambient light, that it is hard to notice sometimes the changing and powerful shifts. On those few nights around the full moon light blasts into my window. I can even sit in that light and feel like I might get a sunburn as if I'm sitting on a beach.

Slowly the light dissipates and disappears. Then for a few weeks, I don't even know that it's not there. But if you've ever been in the desert at night or out in nature, the light of the full moon is unmistakable. As is its absence. The darkness is all-encompassing. In the dark, we can't see as much, but we can see clearer.

My falling-in-love experience was one of those navigating the unknown experiences.

I have never loved so hard, nor had I ever hurt so badly. We didn't break up when he left; we had the sweetest goodbye. I wanted to get on the bus with him for the cross-country trip to get to JFK airport to not over-stay his visa and get deported. He arrived an hour before the flight was set to depart.

I wanted to stay by his side but I watched him go.

As you may remember, the internet in 2006 provided few avenues for international communication, but not many. So when he got home we stayed in touch. After six weeks though he told me we needed to end it.

If you've ever been in love, you know that feeling.
that desolation
when the other person
is not as in as you are.

With the same commitment that I had embraced falling in love, I knew it was time to embrace the sweet agony of breaking up.

It is one thing to be broken up with on the internet; it's an entirely different thing to look someone in the eye and say, "goodbye."

I needed that.

Without much thought or anyone's approval, I bought a ticket to Colombia. Shortly before flying, I told him I was coming. I spoke ten words of Spanish.

If I did not see this first love affair all the way through, I knew I wouldn't quite be able to ever try it again. I would crawl back into the safeguarded lonely place I'd lived my whole life. I got on a plane so he could break up with me to my face. I needed the final nail in the coffin.

What happened then was highly unexpected.

We became friends, true, deep, and genuine friends. To my surprise, we spent a month traveling Colombia in search of a bridge.

You had stood with your family on a stone bridge as a boy.

A long lost photograph had captured a moment in your life. That picture symbolized a time when your family was together and happy. All you had was a memory- and a longing. A village somewhere in Colombia...

So we wandered from town to town. Every village had an old bridge. We saw so many bridges, but none of them were *The Bridge*. Until one day... in a little town in Boyaca, we found *the bridge*. *The bridge that matched not only the photograph but also your memory.*

*The photo that inspired the adventure (*found years later)*

In this process, we got to know each other platonically in a way that we hadn't before because we stumbled into love and sex.

Now it has been almost 20 years since that first visit to Colombia. It took me a few more years to move here *and you know how many more times we broke up, more than six times in five years.* When people hear that I came to Colombia for love and that I've lived here for 14 years and I live as a single mom, they put those pieces together.

That's not how *my* puzzle fits.

I am so glad we met. I'm so glad I came to Colombia so we could break up and become friends.

Now, when people ask how I came to live in Colombia I say, "I came to be broken up with and fell in love with so much more as a result. I fell in love with the country, with a way of life: the culture, the weather, the fruit, and the colors."

It kept pulling me back. Years later I moved to Colombia and taught at a high school. I met another person and had a baby.

But this precious chapter
of my first falling in love

and the sweet agony of falling out of love
over and over again
is one of my favorite chasing-the-moon moments
reaching for something in the dark.
Something that's beyond my fingertips, my footsteps, but
reaching anyway, finding a way forward when there
is no clear or easy path.

Telling the story reminds me that I have it in me to do it again. We all do.

I haven't fallen in love much since then. I have retreated back to the guarded, lonely person where I told myself stories that it's better, safer not to even try, not to be open, to stay safe from love and hurt.

We had fun and love. I even had fun in the heartache. There was something delicious about it. To know that I could fully experience the emotional bandwidth in both directions. It was like seeing in color for the first time or tasting unfamiliar, delicious fruit.

We were just kids. You didn't mean to hurt me. We're all just doing the best that we can. A broken heart isn't something to avoid. The consequences of staying safe are more grave than any heartache. *Thank you for showing me love and devastation in equal measure.*

It's amazing to me still how some seemingly small decisions - whether it was the decision to host a *couchsurfer*
or to cross the room and sit next to you
or the more significant decision to actively and intentionally open my heart. How the simplest little moments can change our lives forever. *I fell in love with you and I gained a country, I gained a language, and a life beyond anything I'd ever imagined for myself. That is a life I am still living today.*

I draft this chapter and share this story in the middle of the night, literally by the light of the moon. With the full moonlight pouring in my window, yet again, the path seems obvious but in a few more days that clarity will fade again, and I will have to move forward regardless, in the dark.

Telling this story reminds me that I have it in me to do it again.

We all do.

With every mystery we are navigating, when we proceed... countless unknown gifts await.

About the Author
Sierra Melcher

Best-selling author, international speaker & educator, Sierra Melcher is founder of **Red Thread Publishing LLC.** She leads an all-female publishing company, with a mission to support 10,000 women to become successful published authors & thought-leaders. Offering world-class coaching & courses that focus on community, collaboration, and a uniquely feminine approach at every stage of the author process.

Sierra has a Master's degree in education, has spoken & taught around the world. Originally from the United States, Sierra lives in Medellin, Colombia with her young daughter.

instagram.com/redthreadbooks
linkedin.com/in/sierra-melcher
amazon.com/author/sierramelcher
goodreads.com/sierra-melcher

Chapter Five

IT GETS BETTER FROM HERE
SHERILLE MARQUEZ

UNEXPECTED BEGINNINGS

If someone had told me that I would be divorced and a single mom at 36, I would have never believed them.

How could this be? I married my best friend. We went to high school together. I loved being with him so much that I would even tag along during his plumbing emergency calls just to sit in the truck so I could be around him.

My sister once told me I lived a Betty Crocker life. She said I was co-dependent, but I didn't know what that meant. I was 19 years old when my ex-husband and I started dating, so I thought I was just in love.

We went to high school together, and our history and friendship made our bond stronger. Everyone viewed us as the 'golden couple,' what you would call #relationshipgoals. We got married when we were both 22, had many friends, and truly enjoyed each other's company.

For as long as I can remember, I've always been incredibly ambitious. I've never allowed anyone or anything to get in the way of achieving my goals. By the time we were 28, we had already bought a second house, started a small plumbing company, and had two kids.

IGNORING THE SIGNS

I was so caught up in chasing my dreams and being in love that I didn't pay attention to important things "mature" people do before marriage. I should have asked myself important questions like, "What are my potential life partner's values, morals, and principles? Do we see eye to eye on finances? How would we raise our children?"

All I cared about was being with my best friend for the rest of my life, and I ignored all the red flags.

The night of our wedding rehearsal, my ex's mother wanted to have a mother-and-son dance. I said, "No problem, please go ahead and arrange it with the DJ." I explained that I wasn't comfortable being in the spotlight with my stepdad but encouraged her to proceed. I didn't think there was anything wrong with what I said, but thanks to her excessive alcohol consumption, it provoked her, and she flipped a switch.

I will never forget her glare as she shouted at me, "I don't want to miss out on anything because of your family hang-ups!"

I froze at that moment, utterly confused by her statement. Hadn't I just given her the green light to arrange the dance with the DJ?

But hold onto your seat because the drama is just getting started!

As the night progressed, things took a turn for the worse. My ex, his out-of-town friend, his mother, and I all carpooled back to my apartment.

I didn't even have enough time to put my car in park when my ex jumped out and took off on foot. To where I had no idea. But this was his way of dealing with difficult situations – walking away without notice or punching walls.

By that point, both his mother and his friend had also exited my car. I was so upset; my head was spinning. All I could think about was finding my ex and calming him down because we were about to get married in less than 24 hours.

His friend and I became a mini search party. By now, we were in the middle of the street at 2 AM. I was in my car, and he was next to me on foot. Our plan was to divide and conquer.

As he and I were trying to figure out which route to take, I felt a car smash into the back of my car. My soon-to-be mother-in-law deliberately ran her car into mine and then took off like a hit-and-run! She later told my ex her intention was "to kill the bride so that there would be no wedding." These words are forever etched in my brain.

That is just one of the many red flags, and they are equally as shocking.

Why did I stay? I was too young, too in love, and too naive to walk away.

A PAINFUL DISCOVERY

We began building our lives, and periodically, we would go through ups and downs, just like any "normal" married couple or people in committed relationships. The period of ups and downs lasted about a decade, then we had a 3-year break before the beginning of the end happened.

Things were very rocky for about a month at this point. He was doing out-of-character things that I thought were just a mid-life crisis.

The night after we got home from Legoland for my son's birthday, he said he was going for a drive. It was 11 PM. He didn't get home until 2 AM. I had my suspicions of another woman by the way he would hold his phone, and take longer showers, but he didn't strike me as someone who would cheat on me.

I love my sleep, and I usually sleep peacefully like a baby. That night was the worst sleep of my life if you can even call it that. My stomach was in knots from all the different scenarios I was imagining of what he could be doing. I ended up taking a dump about 5 times within two hours.

The power of prayer is remarkable and miraculous. I kept praying over and over for God to reveal the truth. Little did I know I was about to experience a miracle.

I heard the sound of the door chime, and it was 2 AM.

The next day I confronted him. It took everything in my power to maintain my composure and not lose it. My heart was pounding so hard I could feel it in my chest.

My intuition said, "Now is the time. There he is, ask him where he was last night." And I did, despite all of the different emotions I was feeling - anger, sadness, and confusion.

He started making small talk with me as if nothing happened. I played along for a couple of minutes and then I blurted out, "So where were you last night?" He said he went driving to clear his head. I said, "Oh really? For three hours?" He said he drove for an hour and a half and stopped to smoke weed and then drove another hour and a half and came home.

I felt as if God was speaking through me: I said, "I don't believe you, let me see your phone." He hesitated for a brief moment and then handed me his phone.

I could feel his gaze as I was scrolling through every text message. It only took the third message to confirm what I had been feeling this whole time—there was another woman, and there was a picture of her ass to prove it.

After I sent myself all the screen captures of their conversation, I chucked his phone on the dining table, and said, "Here you go. I hope it was worth it. Now get your shit and get the fuck out."

Finding out about his affair wasn't even the hardest part. The hardest part was breaking the news to my kids who were ten and seven at the time.

I thought I was going to 1-2-3 the whole divorce since I knew my value, my worth, and what my children and I deserve.

A JOURNEY THROUGH DEPRESSION

The first month I was sitting pretty. I immediately purged my entire house of all memory of him. I didn't hesitate to throw my wedding album away and sold my wedding ring.

I even thought to myself, "Wow, this is not as bad as I thought it was going to be." My friends thought I was an alien because I wasn't sad, and I wasn't breaking down. But then life had other plans.

A month later, the unraveling started. I started eating food like it was going out of style and I couldn't get enough. I wasn't aware that emotional eating took hold of me. I didn't understand why I couldn't get full, how eating became a hobby and why my go-to was chips.

My emotional eating lasted for years. One of the lowest points was when I reached a stage where I no longer trusted myself with food. I would go on "pretend" grocery runs just to indulge in free sample chips and snacks. It wasn't because I couldn't afford it; it was because I didn't trust myself not to eat the whole thing in one sitting.

I didn't even know what depression felt like. I'm a very happy person inherently. The only way I could articulate it when people asked me how I was doing was to describe it as a feeling like there was a dark cloud over me and that I lost my "mojo."

I would be working and staring at the same piece of paper, re-reading the same paragraph for 30 minutes because nothing was sinking in.

During those times, I felt like I was having an out-of-body experience. I felt so lost and disconnected from myself. It was like I was just a shell of a person, but no one knew that because I was good at hiding and pretending that I was doing "good" and smiling through my pain.

I wasn't just lying to everyone, I was lying to myself, because deep down, nothing could be farther from the truth.

ATTRACTING TOXIC RELATIONSHIPS

I was attracting the wrong kinds of guys - the ones who wouldn't even be in my experience if I were in a better place vibrationally. But back then, I was a magnet for men who gave me less than what I deserved. Since I didn't know who I truly was, combined with codependency, I allowed them to stay in my life longer than I normally would.

I spent years in this space of lack and self-doubt, which felt more like purgatory. I was just getting by, even though I held onto my faith. I believed that every January 1st was my comeback year. I felt stuck in survival mode, and my external world reflected the uncertainty, fear, loss, and disempowerment of my inner world.

Just when I didn't think things could get worse, I let someone into my life who proved me wrong.

In the beginning, it was exciting because he was giving me the time and attention I was yearning for. I overlooked all the red flags: he drank too much every day, he didn't have a stable job, he didn't have his own car, and he was 10 years younger than me. I have a very youthful spirit, so it's not uncommon for me to attract younger guys. The real trouble lies in the life stages, and I have a decade's worth of experience with him.

Even though it only lasted 18 months, that relationship was what woke me up and ignited my journey of self-discovery. It was another blessing in disguise which I didn't know at the time.

Being in that relationship brought out the worst in me. It was the most challenging and tumultuous time I've ever had in my entire life.

We argued nearly every day, and I had no respect for him. Because of that, I was careless with my words and very condescending. I allowed him to not only keep me stagnant but also regress. I felt like I was missing out on life, and time with my family, and friends because he was holding me back. I felt stuck.

Even though I wanted out of the relationship so badly, I still found myself clinging to it because it was familiar. I was comfortable having a body there, even if that body was toxic.

Everyone has a limit. I reached mine the day I saw him disheveled after another binge-drinking episode. My kids happened to be with me, which woke me up even more.

OVERCOMING FEAR AND SHAME

There was absolutely no way I was going to have anyone like that around my children. To me, the most important job I could ever have in my entire life is being the best mom I can be. That means that anyone or anything that gets in the way has to go.

That was the moment I made a decision that I was going to do whatever it took to rebuild myself and my children's lives even better than when I was married.

I didn't know how I was going to do it. I had absolutely no plan. But what I did know is that I needed to kick this motherfucker out of my house.

That night, I cried so hard. I felt so much shame for finding myself in this place again. How could it happen to someone who always strived to make the "right" choices? How did I reach this level of desperation and codependency, allowing someone to drain me for so long?

If you've ever faced hardships in life, there comes a moment in your journey when you say, "Enough is enough." You refuse to continue feeling this way. You refuse to watch life pass you by as you do nothing. You no longer want to live in fear and shame, worrying about what others might think of you for failing again.

At that point, I stopped caring about being judged. My priority was cleaning up my life, no matter what it took or how long it would take to get there.

After my divorce, life relentlessly knocked me down for several years. But no matter how battered and bruised I felt, no matter how many times I hit the ground, I always found the strength to rise again. My warrior spirit simply wouldn't accept defeat.

It reminds me of my favorite speech by Theodore Roosevelt "The Man in the Arena."

This speech deeply resonates with me because I am that woman in the arena. Life has thrown its hardest punches, but I refuse to stay down. Each tough lesson I've learned has become a stepping stone, propelling me toward the next stage of my growth.

RISING FROM DIVORCE ASHES

Let me be candid: the journey of self-discovery and reinvention is not easy. It demands everything from you and more. But amidst the darkness, the human spirit clings to hope, believing in the possibility of transformation and a brighter tomorrow.

I've learned that resilience is something deep inside us, waiting to be tapped into when things get tough. It's what keeps us going when everything seems hopeless. Resilience isn't passive; it's an active force that helps us adapt and thrive in difficult situations.

But resilience alone isn't enough. We also need a growth mindset – believing in our ability to learn and improve. Instead of seeing challenges as roadblocks, I've learned to see them as opportunities for personal growth reinforcing my belief that life is always happening FOR us, not TO us.

Making choices is another powerful tool for overcoming challenges. Every decision we make, no matter how small, can shape our future. By making intentional choices aligned with our values, we can reinvent our paths and take control of our lives.

I spent years in self-study, trial and error until I discovered my own answers. Not once did I allow my hardships to make me bitter. Instead, I used it as a springboard to make me better. I transmuted the pain and suffering into purpose and became a beacon of hope and empowerment for divorced women and single moms.

A BEACON OF HOPE

Today, I'm recognized as a thought leader and leading expert in the field of transformational coaching for divorced women. I have appeared in several top-rated podcasts, featured in magazine articles, and named "Top 20 Women Entrepreneurs to Take Inspiration from in 2024" by Entrepreneurs Herald, and now a published author!

I've always known my purpose in life was to help others. However, when your purpose becomes bigger than you, it becomes a calling. After reinventing myself and rebuilding my and my children's lives I felt a calling to give back to address the needs of divorced women struggling with identity and moving their lives forward.

By integrating empirical-based science, spirituality, and alternative healing modalities, I am able to help my clients bring about deep change by overcoming self-sabotaging limiting beliefs, negative self-talk patterns, and emotional blocks getting in the way of feeling confident and loving themselves wholeheartedly. I teach them how to organize their thoughts effectively and help assess their restrictive thought patterns that block their forward momentum to their goal and move them to a growth mindset where permanent change occurs.

What took me almost a decade to learn, I now teach my clients in 90 days or less. If you're ready to reclaim your power and design a life even better than before, I invite you to send me an email and reserve your seat for my free workshop, "Biohacking Your Best Life After Divorce."

As I embark on this new chapter, I'm grateful for the strength and wisdom I've gained from facing adversity. My journey has taught me that resilience, a growth mindset, and empowered choices are key to navigating life's ups and downs.

If you find yourself facing tough times, remember this: embrace your resilience, have faith in your capacity to grow, and make choices that empower you. Every challenge presents an opportunity for growth and transformation. Your past doesn't define you; it's the groundwork for crafting a brighter future. You hold the power to reinvent yourself and your life, no matter your age.

Until we meet again, keep rising!

About the Author
Sherille Marquez

Sherille Marquez, a thought leader, author, and founder, guides divorced women through transformative changes, drawing inspiration from her own journey of overcoming a devastating divorce while raising two boys. Despite consulting with three therapists, a crucial element was missing, propelling Sherille into years of self-study and trial and error. After rebuilding her life and those of her children, she felt a calling to give back, addressing the needs of divorced women struggling with identity and moving their lives forward.

Sherille stands as a beacon of hope and empowerment for those navigating the challenges of post-divorce life. Integrating empirical-based science, spirituality, and alternative healing modalities, she facilitates comprehensive transformations, recognizing the profound impact of divorce on a woman's total health. Sherille strives to redefine the narrative of life after divorce, proving that through self-discovery and empowerment, every woman can craft a life on her terms—a life not just survived but passionately lived.

linktr.ee/coachsherille

Chapter Six

HOPE WAS BORN THAT NIGHT
KRISTINA GREEN

T he night always brought about a healthy dose of self-reflection and memories of a life not yet achieved. It was the time my mind had its field day with my emotions, tallying up the missteps of adult decisions while still a 'child' myself. I was only twenty-three and midway through college when my son was born. Yep, I was on the slow track working full-time and taking classes in the evening.

One evening that sticks out amongst so many was the night I nearly gave up on my future. It was late and I had lost all my steam from burning the candle on both ends as they say. Tired from a day of shuffling between the responsibilities of caring for my now one-year-old son and navigating a full-time job as a single mom, I was simply exhausted, and I hadn't any fight left in me.

My job was flexible, and deadlines were reasonable, but I was not accustomed to balance. I was still sending emails at midnight and stealing moments away from my son to work on projects, hoping to get more than five hours of sleep each night. The thought of adding one more item to my ever-growing "to-do" list was terrifying and that night it was time for me to register to return to the university. Having taken two semesters off and with nearly sixty units remaining (about two years) I was so close but still so far from achieving a dream that was to change my stars.

Flashing back a year, it was the start of what should have been my senior year at the university when I saw a "+" indicated on the home test. I was pregnant. At the age of twenty-two, many would have been devastated by this news, but I was delighted. Delusional and unaware of the long road ahead, yes, but delighted, nonetheless. I was fulfilling a lifelong dream of becoming a mom. Okay, perhaps I hadn't imagined it would happen quite like this, but nothing would overshadow my excitement for this new life that was now in my protection.

Kristina Green, April, 2002

Once I got the nerve to tell my mom she asked me, ever so cautiously, how I felt about the news. I expressed my delight and she sighed with relief. I could always count on my mom to be supportive. Although sooner than she would have imagined, she was thrilled to become a grandmother. There was nothing to be done except prepare for the arrival of the young man who would forever change my life.

Having children was the only future I was certain about. The thought of college terrified me. I felt like I was a sure failure just waiting for the next assignment or exam to demolish me and prove my greatest fears that I just wasn't cut out for it. Although I was an A and B student, I felt like I was going through the motions and barely getting by. Career-wise I had no idea what I wanted to pursue but I always knew that I wanted children. Okay, maybe not midway through college but there was no changing the timing. This was happening.

I took a temporary position conducting telephone outreach at a national health insurer. It was only a two-week assignment, but I was grateful for the work. The assignment was working evenings to make outbound calls to members. I exceeded my quotas and impressed the right people because that was the beginning of my twenty-plus-year career in healthcare.

Hired full-time as a customer service representative, I was within months of delivering my son. Balancing work, school, and an ever-growing responsibility in my belly I pretended like it was all going to be just fine. Aside from morning sickness, my pregnancy was ideal and my day-to-day was not greatly impacted.

Sure, I would have cravings for chocolate milkshakes and French apple pie practically daily, a craving I quickly had to limit. I once called nearly every restaurant within a ten-mile radius in search of a French apple pie - not to be mistaken for a Dutch apple pie - and nearly drove everyone crazy with my interrogations. You see, the difference is in the topping of the pie. A Dutch apple pie is crumbly while a French apple pie has a top crust. A distinction that was beyond important to the ever-growing pregnant me around five months.

Yes, the pregnancy crazies got me in their clutches, and boy was it fun. I know I drove my family nuts but when else do you practically get a free pass to be a little extra? Exactly! I milked all that attention by accepting every offer to "make a run" or "pick me up something on the way." I didn't discriminate. If they were offering, I was accepting.

By all accounts, I was doing well. I had achieved the job security I needed and was managing four classes at the university. I was curbing my cravings and preparing to take my finals mere weeks before my due date of June 22, 2002.

I went on to have a smooth delivery and quickly settled into my new role as a mama, protector, and provider for my son, Michael. A role I was in love with from the start. My son gave me purpose and taught me the meaning of "mother's love." A concept that I had only heard about and superficially understood, but never had the experience. I was honored to be entrusted with such an important responsibility and would do my best to live up to every depiction of mothering I had witnessed.

Having taken a year off from the university, it was now time for me to register to return. A moment I had been dreading since I had my son. I had been avoiding this moment since I received the registration notification. The party was officially coming to an end for my future was calling me to reprioritize and get back to work on my degree. I was in mourning because I knew this meant that a sacrifice was on the horizon.

The thought of juggling the sacrifice between a full-time job, being a new mama, and now school was a daunting task. How was I expected to prioritize? Nothing was more important than my new baby boy. He deserved more of me than anything else, but I knew a sacrifice - albeit temporary - was inevitable. So, I ignored the dreadful feeling of a future littered with missed "firsts" and focused on a life of experiences and opportunities that would prove to be worth it. One day he would understand, and I would make him proud.

It was late and I had just put my son to sleep while trying to make sense of an endless course catalog of classes. I was in search of evening courses to satisfy my graduation requirements while also minimizing the impact on my work schedule. I was beginning to feel overwhelmed at the thought of squeezing a school schedule into my life that was already jam-packed with responsibilities. With each passing moment, I was building a plan and orchestrating time away from my son, which made me feel like I was scheming and curbing my responsibilities as a mom. Perhaps it was postpartum blues but that feeling never subsided. To this day, I know I did the right thing and I still carry a sense of regret for having to make that choice.

Hopelessness was my primary emotion as I weighed the options on both sides of the scale of whether to return to school or put my baby first and be a mom. The more I considered the sacrifice the more I wanted no part of a plan that would pull me from my child. My future was entrapped with the idea that a degree was required for the future I wanted and deserved. An entire future predicated on the achievement of my degree was slowly starting to slip away. Something that neither of my parents had completed and therefore had reached a ceiling to their success because of it. That degree meant freedom and limitless possibilities and held the keys to my future, and I was somehow still stuck weighing the options.

The dream of becoming who I was meant to be was fading away as I watched the time pass and my registration window close. I had a small window - about two to four hours - to dial into the registration phone line, input the requested course numbers, and listen for either an acceptance or a notification that I was waitlisted. I instead chose inaction and just sat there as time passed and eventually closed. With the stroke of the completion of the final moment for registration, I had cast a vote for my future through my inaction because I did not register for even one class.

In that moment there was sadness and a sense of defeat that came over me for I had just let my future slip away without a fight. Not because I was preoccupied or even distracted but because I was simply overwhelmed and afraid of the challenge that lay ahead. I saw the road before me and was doubtful of my capabilities because I was scared I would fail, and I was therefore unwilling to even try. I felt like I wasn't made of the right stuff to be successful, and as I lived out each of those moments, I believed those words to be true.

That night was no different, I was at a crossroads, and I had to make a decision. While my future hung in the balance, I watched life flow in and out of my son with each rise and fall of his chest. The moonlight illuminated his face ever so gently as he lay on his back with not a care or awareness of the turmoil that was brewing inside me. I cried into my pillow as I watched my son almost as if for approval to feel and experience the fullness of the despair of that moment. Trying so hard not to vocalize my pain, I buried my face in my pillow as if to silence the trumpeting reality of my defeat.

Through my despair, my thoughts took me well into the future where I was having a hypothetical conversation with my son, now in his teens and preparing for his next phase of life. We were in a heated discussion about college, and I was insistent on his attending, and he was expressing his desire otherwise. I felt unqualified to hold my position because in this future I had not graduated. I had become the failure that I had feared and now my son was following in my footsteps, and I had nothing to say. I was simply devastated.

Still lying in my bed with this new image of what the future held for both me and my son, I felt a pull and an awakening that this was not what my life was to become. I was meant for much more than a moment of despair could ever deliver. I was stronger than the emotions of this moment and it was time to live up to my potential. My eyes still wet from self-pity, I arose with a renewed sense of purpose and motivation. I could not consider for one moment giving up and disappointing the future 'Me' or my son.

I worked tirelessly into the early morning concocting a series of plans to right the wrongs of the events earlier in the evening. I was not giving up and I was not going to be a disappointment. I was going to be an example for my son and that moment started now. In the end, classes were secured, I was enrolled in the university again, and yes, I was absent for some *firsts*. But I was also present for so many moments and carry memories that melt my heart to this day.

Although it was the hardest decision I had made up to that point, it was the right choice for our future. My degree allowed me to have access to promotions that were otherwise closed to me. Doors opened because I had achieved the minimum barrier to entrance, a degree. A concept that is starting to fade away these days with a lesser focus on academic achievement and a greater focus on personal branding. However, that degree bridged the gap and launched my career in healthcare administration where I learned to be an accountable leader and thought partner. An experience that I would not trade for anything else for it has shaped me into the person I have become and blessed me with the experience of supporting so many through their career and life transitions.

Hope was born that night, under a full bright moon carrying whispers of dreams yet to be fulfilled. The hope for something more and the dream that was still to come. We are often tested with pivotal moments of despair and disappointment in our lives. It is in these moments that we discover our truth and while we may turn away from our dreams at times, we can always find our way back. Our dreams live within us and mold and reshape over time to align with the future we are manifesting.

While in one of the lowest moments of my life, I rediscovered my purpose through the eyes of my son. I had reached the peak of my test and thought I had given up, but instead, I gave myself permission to change my mind. You see, we often think that we have to commit to only one path and once we start moving along that path, we think we cannot stop or change directions. The burden of proceeding along a journey that no longer suits you will grow a mass of resentment within you. Joy and happiness are not found through living a life of obligation but rather through the pursuit of love and kindness.

One decision to choose a different path, to reject hopelessness, and to recognize my power of choice are what saved me that night. I gave myself permission to have hope, to have fear and uncertainty, and to also not accept despair and disappointment as my fate. I had more power than I knew. Life was kicking me down, but it was not happening to me. Life was orchestrating options, and I had the power to choose any of them. I chose to be more than my perceived limitations and disadvantages and chose to believe that my story was waiting for me to show up.

Someone is waiting for you to show up and be your authentic self. She has watched you take second, third, and even last place in your life and yet she waits patiently in the shadows for you to see her and to acknowledge her. It is then she is confident that that one time will spark a light in you both that will forever guide your path. She is waiting for the 'You' that is buried deep inside to feel the warmth of the sun on your face and the inspirational light of the moon in your midst. To feel the blossoming of possibilities that await you both simply by showing up exactly as you are to step out of the shadows and into all you are meant to become. No more hiding; simply living your truth and all the fumbling beautiful mess it is.

Her silence is your suffering. How long will you keep her waiting?

About the Author
Kristina M Green

Kristina M Green is an author, women empowerment speaker, and career strategy coach. She specializes in helping marginalized women take up space and feel confident in every room by empowering them to take incremental steps towards a dream they never realized was attainable. To do what scares them so that they can experience the reality of their dreams now.

linktr.ee/kristinamgreen

Chapter Seven

IF NOT NOW, WHEN?

JESSICA GOLDMUNTZ STOKES

"*I have to leave. I have to quit my job.....*"
The gut punch of this message shook me to my core. Leaving was not just a matter of giving a 2-week notice, I was part-owner of a company and the operating manager. It's complicated to extract myself.

But the message was so strong. It permeated my body. It rippled through me, tingling my toes, filling me up, like shock waves. It bursted from me. I think I felt it in the outer edges of my aura.

The hit of intuition was big. Bigger than most, and I have had plenty of intuitive, gut-knowing messages. I don't always listen, but I know if I stop and pay attention, the knowledge of these messages is all around. Waiting to be heard.

A second message whispered.

"*But I like my job...*"

That afternoon started a journey of deep self-reflection and soul-searching. It forced me to examine and look at the choices I had made over the past 15 years. Actually, in the past 40 years. How did I get here? How do any of us arrive at where we are?

I like to think that I was intentional on my professional journey, but I was not at all.

Many of my choices seemed to present themselves to me, and eager to try new things, I saw each one as an adventure. Like turning a page in a choose-your-own-adventure story, I let the next career move fall into the path and embraced it to be the best next thing.

This 'skill' became a strength professionally, and I was able to dynamically pivot and gain new business or new opportunities. In turn, I grew our business, and we were quite successful. I continued to learn, and it was fun. And the stories I have to tell...

Over the 15 years we have owned the business, I have questioned if I wanted to be where I was several times. But something would happen, a new opportunity, or unknown prospects of what else I would or could do. Or just that feeling of safety of not making a big move.

"If not now, when?" That bold voice that was determined to be heard smacked me upside my head.

If not now, when? I was not getting any younger. I have always heaped my proverbial plate full of too many servings. I like all the activities I do. I want to do more. There is always something on my to-do list. I have absolutely no idea what it is like to be bored. My husband teases me: if a bit of room opens up on that plate, I just move everything else around, finding more room for more. My plate is always spilling over in activities. I burn the flame at both ends. I am way too stressed out. I need to slow down.

I needed a break. I needed to rest. I needed to clear the plate.

I needed to leave my job.

It was time to give room to some of those other activities, I needed to honor the other aspects that bring me joy. It was time to clear the room on my plate, and even though I love what I do, it was time.

My Mom taught me about intuition when I was just eight years old. I am certain she did not know she was doing so, but she gave me a true sense of listening to those intuitive 'hits' and trusting myself. Mom studied and learned about energy fields, chakras, meditation, and intuition in her studies of Therapeutic Touch.

Therapeutic Touch (TT) is defined in the Merriam-Webster online dictionary as follows: "a technique in alternative medicine that involves passing the hands over the body of the person being treated and that is held to induce relaxation, reduce pain, and promote healing." *Developed in the 70's, with its foundation in nursing, Mom studied with the founder Dora Kunz and Delores Krieger in the early years. Mom both practiced and then taught Therapeutic Touch. As she learned, I learned. I was a receptive vessel. I loved it. I thrived in her knowledge and her willingness to share with me.

These days, many of us have mindfulness apps on our phones. Maybe we have been introduced to meditation and deep breathing as a common tool to navigate anxiety, depression, and general health.

And likely, many of us have had some exposure to massage, chiropractic, acupuncture, or energy work in some modality.

Certainly, in the late 70's an influx of awareness was blooming. Mom embraced it.

Not only did she practice with our entire family, but she shared her learnings with me and kept the door of my own intuitive abilities wide open. As a child, I didn't even know that there was a door to close on my intuition and my psychic abilities.

I truly think all children have some intuitive and psychic abilities. Often, we (society) shut it out. We tell children that their imaginary friend is pretending or that the 'gut feeling' they have is wrong. What if those imaginary friends are their support and guides? What if we taught children to trust their gut?

The first element or step of Therapeutic Touch is to be centered or grounded. One achieves this by quieting the mind, letting go of the excess clutter in our mind or finding a place of quiet and mindfulness. Meditation. (There's an app for that....)

I must have been about seven or eight when my Mom taught me how to find a state of groundedness. When she started teaching, she had a way to guide people to feel this state of center. She practiced this with my brother, my cousins and me. She would lead people in a guided meditation. It started by having us take deep breaths. She would lead her students to imagine the feeling of the grounded roots of a tree and the calm stillness as they watch the water on the surface of a pond. She had us imagine roots coming out of our feet and reaching within the earth.

In TT, the center of your hands becomes your guidepost and a beacon. They are your tools in assessing someone's energy field. Mom would end her meditation by having us put our hands together, like in prayer. She would then tell us to breathe and connect with the awareness between our hands and pull our hands apart, focusing on our palms. Often, there is intense awareness and a sensation that is felt between your hands. People have a variety of experiences when they explore this activity. Your energy may present itself as a temperature: warm, hot, or cold. The pull of energy between your hands may feel like taffy being pulled apart or it may present as a color. Other ways you can feel may include a sensation of waves of energy, opposing magnets pulling at one another or like a vibration between your palms. Language is limiting in describing what can happen. We do not have the words that can be translated. I usually feel a tingly jolt of connection and a deep sensation or vibration that I am plugged in. The best way to describe it is a 'zing' or a 'buzz.'

When Mom taught her classes, this would lead to a variety of exercises to continue to explore and understand energy flow. For me, as a child, this activity taught me how to 'know' and how to 'see.'

And I was 'seeing', a lot. Mom and I discovered my natural ability (again, I think many children have this) to see auras by accident. Casually, she broached the subject. Around the same time. I was eight.

"Jess, when you look at me what do you see?" Mom asked me this open-ended question, positioning me to answer.

"What do you mean? What do I see? I see you?" I did see my Mom. I did not know it, but I saw not only her physical body but her energy too. This was just the way my vision took in what was presented. I saw (and see) auras.

"No, what do you see around me? Do you see anything?" Mom touched the edge of her arm and pulled up away from her physical skin. "What do you see? Out here?"

"I see you. What do you mean? Of course, I see your arm." I placed my hand on her arm and showed her. And then I pulled it away and declared, "We all have colors around us. You don't see that?"

I saw her in her entirety. And for me, at eight, I didn't know that most people didn't see colors around people. I didn't know I was seeing her aura. I saw people in circles. Their full radiance shines beyond the physical constraints of their bodies. (I was shook.)

Mom was quiet. I did not know how to respond. So, I became quiet too. She was my Mom. My everything. I played off her cues.

"You see colors? Out here?" She vaguely drew a line around her body, touching her skin, but pointing a few inches from her skin.

"All around", I insisted. Confused and in awe. What was she talking about? There was skin, and there were colors. To my eight-year-old mind, this was crazy. People were colors. That was that. What was my mom talking about?

After that, Mom & I would have many conversations about what I saw. She was never judgmental, always curious. She always encouraged me to be present with myself and my explorations. She never shut down my visual acuity or my sensing of energy.

Strangely, it helped her. Although she was teaching and practicing mindfulness and had a deep connection with TT, she would continue to say she felt very little energetically through most of her time practicing. Those receiving always felt her warmth and relief from her work. She loved talking and sharing with me and together, we explored energy.

Another key element of practicing TT is setting the intention to help and heal. Mom embraced this and taught me to be clear that we were supporting people on their own journey of self-healing. We were just conduits of people's ability to heal themselves.

In Junior High, when all kids are embracing lots of emotions, I became overwhelmed with the amount of energy going on around me. Mom encouraged me to find a way to 'protect myself' by surrounding myself with a sphere of white translucent or golden light. Together, we discovered a way for me to 'turn off' my sensing too much energy. It is hard to explain how we crafted this intention or idea. The basis of it is like turning down the volume on your speaker. The frequency becomes lower.

In College, I took a one credit 'conversation' course on Meditation, and I realized I had been practicing and doing a version of mindfulness since I was eight when Mom taught me about TT and energy fields.

Around this time, I intuitively knew my life would someday involve this type of work. It was not just the energetic skills Mom taught me; she coached me how to work with it. How to listen to my inner knowing, my inner voice. Through the work we did, I innately knew of my intuition.

Yet, I often did not listen. I would be dismissive of the knowing, justifying it in a variety of ways. Telling myself I was not ready or that eventually when, someday, maybe, I would explore the 'calling.' I suppose I wasn't. My life took me many other interesting professional and personal paths. All the while, there was a small nagging pull that someday I would do more with those skills, 'when I grew up.'

"If not now, when."

Listening is often a challenge. So, this time, at 52, when that nagging intuitive "hit" smacked me upside the head, I finally listened and started the process and journey of leaving my job and imagining what comes next.

It has not been smooth. And it is not done yet. Growth and journeys are not straightforward paths. This I know. I explore this in my book, *Seeking Clarity in the Labyrinth, a Daughter's Journey Through Alzheimer's.* In it, I use the labyrinth pattern and specifically, the one that Mom and Aunt Joyce built in my parents' backyard, to illustrate that life and all the complexities associated with life are not straight lines.

It's time to quit my 'day job'? I have always had a healthy (sometimes financially satisfying) dose of a secondary income. I have published books, I have taught Therapeutic Touch, I do Reiki, and have done multiple workshops regarding Labyrinths. I also teach belly dancing. I have always loved and thrived in my other passions.

But, letting go of the 'day job'. This is very new and hard. Uncomfortable. I like what I have done, and it is also time to let go. That yearning and knowledge from my youth is percolating and presenting itself in new ways. I MUST go explore.

I have to.

When Mom died in January 2022, a few days before she transitioned, Dad & I spent the most magical day with her. I did TT on her, ending by holding her feet, helping her become centered, or grounded. Just like Mom taught me when I was eight years old. It was comforting to share and gift back to her a technique that has become so accessible to me. For Mom, there was a settling and knowing as I connected with her. Although language was gone, we still had a way to communicate. With our energy. With our hands.

I must go explore this more. The calling isn't a whisper anymore but has urgency. Direction. Like the pull of waves in an ocean on a full moon. It is time.

Since publishing my book in January of 2023 (one year after Mom's passing), I have named the labyrinth Mom and Joyce built. I call it our Legacy Labyrinth. My favorite time to walk is in the moonlight. It is the most special time when the rocks are kissed in the sublime light of a full moon, or when it is barely visible in the darkness of the new moon. Both times, with hidden visions and promises.

As I embark on my new life, I imagine that the legacy of my work will be intricately woven into all the ways Mom gifted me skills over the years, I will find my path. It likely will not be pretty. My nature will fight it. There will still be uphill mountains to climb. I also imagine it will be laced with all the things that were Mom. Labyrinths and energy work likely will be at the center. Teaching and giving to others will be present as well.

Intuitively, my heart will always feel Mom walking with me. Perhaps, at 52, I am grown up. Now it is time to embrace my wisdom and, most perfectly, walk by the light of the moon.

Please visit my website, www.JessicaStokesAuthor.com for information on upcoming events and a downloadable Labyrinth Workbook.

About the Author
Jessica Goldmuntz Stokes

Best-selling author, speaker, and educator Jessica Goldmuntz Stokes is an entrepreneur at heart. Always seeking her own growth and truth, she teaches and performs belly dance and practices therapeutic touch and Reiki. She is a daughter, a mom, a wife, a friend, and a caregiver. She has navigated multiple family members with Alzheimer's, dementia, and Parkinson's. She is an avid labyrinth-walker, a trained Veriditas Labyrinth facilitator, and a published author of *Seeking Clarity in the Labyrinth, A Daughter's Journey Through Alzheimer's*. She also contributed to the anthology *Planting the Seed: Lessons to Cultivate a Brighter Future* and *Notes from Motherland: The Wild Adventures of Raising Humans*. She provides Labyrinth workshops, lectures, and retreats for anyone experiencing change, loss, or growth.

linktr.ee/jagstokes

Chapter Eight

THE LAWSUIT

ALICE STARK

In 2018 I thought I had finally landed my dream job. After decades of working for mostly ungrateful bosses and passionless projects, I was elated to find a role in a cannabis startup that combined perfectly my passion for the industry that was finally legalized in Canada in 2016, in addition to my experience and skills in project management. This sounds like the perfect cover letter sentence, doesn't it? I found the job posting serendipitously and I was hired quickly as my new boss saw that I could contribute beyond my planned role and put me in charge of a strategic project that would have me work closely with the CEO. I was on cloud nine. I felt like I was finally being rewarded by the cosmos with the perfect opportunity for me. I woke up every day and went to work with a sense of newfound purpose. Within one month of starting, I was congratulated and recognized in front of the whole company for bringing the CEO's vision to life so quickly. It turns out that when something seems too good to be true it likely is.

Within a month, the honeymoon period quickly and unexpectedly ended when I was forced to work with a hostile contractor hired by the most influential VP. At first, I excitedly welcomed the help because there was a lot of pressure to deliver on my project. The contractor was experienced and, if we could work effectively together, it would help me divide and conquer. Soon however I learned that the contractor was assigned to my project because none of the people who he was hired to work with initially wanted to work with him due to his attitude. Instead of firing him and admitting that his choice was ineffective, the VP implanted him firmly in my project. For the purpose of this story, I will call the contractor Napoleon as it became quickly obvious that he had a raging Napoleon complex. After weeks of trying to work with Napoleon, he started to try and pressure me with constant harassment instead of actually helping me. So not only was he not contributing to the project but he was actively trying to undermine my efforts and discredit my work behind my back. Before our issue escalated, he often complained to me that the project was unrealistic and, as he realized we might not be able to deliver it, he wanted to put the blame squarely on me and salvage his reputation.

I am a very direct person so I asked Napoleon explicitly to cease and desist from being negative and stop harassing me for deliverables that I was not accountable for. I purposely asked this in writing in case I needed it documented for escalation with HR. I asked my manager and Napoleon's VP for us all to meet and align on our roles and responsibilities as the current working relationship was untenable. At that point, my manager who had sung my praises for the last two months started icing me out. I had become a problem that he was not equipped to deal with. Napoleon's superior was a VP with more experience and influence. He manipulated my manager into seeing me as the problem. In a last attempt to garner some empathy and resolution, I met with HR and my boss. In tears, I told them that I needed their help to protect my mental health as Napoleon was continuing to trespass professional boundaries despite the meetings we had had. Start-ups tend to hire younger employees for roles that require years of experience. In their managerial immaturity, they treated me like I was hysterical, hoping that if they simply ignored me, I would eventually go away - the definition of gaslighting.

For the next few weeks, nothing was resolved. All my life I had practiced keeping my composure and resilience in the face of bullies. I took copious amounts of CBD oil to balance my nervous system just to make it through each day. Being strong day after day just to start over the next day is exhausting. I was emotionally spent. I did not want to be strong just to make someone else comfortable. I wanted to be safe and vulnerable. I wanted everyone to know my authentic feelings. I sat empty-eyed in meetings and, if someone dared ask me how things were going, I exploded in tears and shared my situation at the expense of professional appearances. I no longer cared what anyone thought. I was the victim so why should I hide myself to make management comfortable and legitimize their incompetence? After the lack of resolution from HR, I couldn't continue functioning on the brink of a mental breakdown. I would have to leave to preserve my sanity. I issued an ultimatum to management: it was me or Napoleon. They had until that same Friday to make a decision or I would quit.

I will never forget going to work on that fateful Friday morning of the ultimatum. I dragged myself out of bed and went to work with a sense of impending doom. As I walked into the office, I felt empty. I had no more fight in me. Whatever the decision would be, it would set me free from this emotional roller coaster. I wanted my peace of mind back. My boss arrived shortly after me and asked me to step into the small meeting room where the HR manager was already waiting. He avoided eye contact and awkwardly blurted out that my previously lauded services would no longer be needed. A few days short of my three-month probation period, I was dismissed.

In that moment, as a pit sunk into my stomach at being wrongfully let go, my heart and mind leaped with joy. A strange freedom had come knocking at my door. As I meandered home in a daze, between bouts of tears of rage I realized that now the power was firmly in my hands. I might have lost the first act of the battle, but now I had the opportunity to win the war. If I had simply quit I would have had to walk away without any further recourse. Being dismissed after flagging harassment with HR meant that now I had cause to sue my ex-employer while receiving government support. That same day I called an old boss and he quickly confirmed my views and referred me to a labor lawyer that I had on retainer by the following week.

∾

The timing of the lawsuit occurred during one of the hardest periods of my life. At the time, I felt very much alone. I didn't speak to my immediate family and I had just ended a nine-year relationship. Yet I will always look back at this decision as one of the most rewarding of my life. Moments of deep trauma are when you really understand the extent of your power and ability to define your own destiny. The way I chose to handle the harassment and lawsuit was a true test of my courage to stand up for myself. After more than two decades of working and saving diligently, I was in the privileged position of being able to pursue justice and pay it forward to those less fortunate. This would be a foundational milestone in my journey of setting boundaries and standing up metaphorically to the bullies who had been gaslighting me since the school playground.

Luckily leading up to the dismissal and lawsuit, I had moved into an airy apartment alone. This became a much-needed sanctuary during this transitional period. Here, I took the time to rest and mourn the past. I had resolved to not let the trauma of the dismissal and lawsuit set in and jade me. I wasn't going to blame or judge myself. I had done the best I could with the information and resources I had. As an Aries moon, I have to honor my sacred rage instead of repressing it. I have to learn from it, get it out and let it go. The unjust dismissal brought to its culmination a process I started long ago to eradicate fear from my body. If the body is a temple, then no one erects temples to fear. That's a recipe for an unbalanced and unhappy life. To let go of the accumulated trauma, I cried a lot over those weeks and the catharsis itself was potent with healing. Tears of mourning pooled in a puddle at my feet daily and my watery eyes reflected back, smiling with release. Emotionally, I felt like a lonely mermaid and I reveled in it. I wished to be soft and sad until my tears were dry.

I had been bullied from an early age and as I learned how to overcome my fear and fight back, I understood the importance of embodying confidence and strength in self-preservation. Just like the king of the jungle, I know what it takes to mark and protect my territory - myself.

To Embody: to give a body to (a spirit), incarnate.

To inspire confidence in myself, I have to embody control of my emotions and courage even if I am petrified inside. The idea of embodying that which inspires me with strength and motivation has been a very powerful self-hypnosis technique for me to overcome my fears over the years. It is an effective strategy in rewriting your internal script and I intentionally harnessed its power during the traumatic dismissal episode.

The only real ally I had at work before I was dismissed was a young developer who introduced me serendipitously to a book called The Master and Margarita. He told me that I was just like the heroine Margarita, free-thinking and courageous. I read the book and, inspired, decided to channel Margarita the warrior witch during the harassment episode. Margarita refuses to be controlled by others' opinions and trusts her own eyes and gut instead to complete her mission. I chose the warrior witch archetype because I identify closely with its energy, and its fierceness is easy to embody. When I headed project meetings with Napoleon and the hostile managers present, I prepared like a soldier going off to war. I cleaned my face, looked at myself in the mirror and bared my teeth like a wolf, grunting and channeling pure animal power. I wore black from head to toe, with leather paneling on my chest like armor. During those meetings, no one dared break the silence in the room before I spoke or challenged me openly. I was the leader of the pack. I felt more powerful in those moments than I ever had. Embodying Margarita, I felt resilient and confident that I inspired fear instead of succumbing to its pull inside.

Lawsuits like mine were usually settled in mediation. When I asked my lawyer how long of a process I should prepare for, she said around five months. I was impatiently looking forward to putting the case behind me but the courts were slow. However, there were signs that inspired me with the confidence that I would win the case sooner than later. For one, the mediation session was set less than a month from submission. It was set to take place on the next full moon. The full moon signifies the completion of a cycle, a fitting omen that this chapter of my life would draw to its conclusion. Still, I was constantly fighting a constant pit of anxiety forming in my stomach and trying to stay positive. A great way to gain confidence is to learn from the warriors who have gone before us. A few days before the mediation, I met with an ex-colleague who had also sued her employer and won. I had always admired her as a mentor. She shared with me the details of her case which further cemented my confidence that I was on the right side of history and that I just needed to keep grounded and focused until I won.

On the morning of the mediation, I tried to remain calm and focused. I used breathwork to slow down my heart rate from exploding in my chest. A warrior witch in control of the elements. Another sign that inspired me with confidence in winning was that only the VP of Finance was present from my ex-employer's side. He was barely familiar with the case, so maybe he was here to just sign my settlement cheque? Positive thoughts, breathe, stay positive. Before the mediation started, my lawyer asked me if I had spent any additional funds on therapy since we last spoke so she could add it to the settlement claim. I looked at her puzzled and responded with unwavering conviction: "You are my therapy. You are going to win this for me. This is the only therapy I need."

The mediation lasted all day as the opposing lawyer bluffed in order to try and corner me but I was positive that I would win. I almost wished I was my own lawyer. No one can possibly fight harder than me for me, know the relevant details of the case better than me. After a day spent in a boardroom waiting impatiently, the mediator finally brought in a decent settlement that I accepted. I was free!

Months after the settlement, poetic justice started unfolding. I received a message from the HR manager of my ex-employer seeking my advice in a case of sexual harassment against the same employer. It turns out management had remained brazen even after my case and had refused to help another employee when she brought the charges forward. I knew that in the eyes of the law, all the facts were on her side and she would win without a doubt. I gave her the only thing she really needed: the confidence to overcome her fears and doubts, the knowledge that she was not alone and that she would win, which she did. Many more months passed. The CEO sold the company and was quickly relieved of his position by the new owners. I saw him months later at a cannabis event. He didn't even recognize me and, best of all, he was unrecognizable. He had already been skinny before but he had managed to lose even more weight since losing his startup, his baby. I like to think that I was part of his karma as he was part of mine. All that remains now are the lessons that serve me, the trauma is long released.

The dismissal also allowed me to receive government support over the next year so I could focus on my business venture in cannabis. A few weeks after the lawsuit had settled, I attended a cannabis industry event as a self-employed entrepreneur. The company that dismissed me was in the cannabis space and the CEO often attended these events. I was dreading the possibility of running into him but instead, I bumped into a friendly ex-colleague familiar with my situation. He had witnessed my tears at work and now he commented on how much happier I seemed since I left. I was ecstatic to hear this as I felt in alignment with my life's purpose for the first time in a very long time. I knew I was on the right path. Hearing him reflect my joy to me was all the validation I needed that I had made the right decisions for the person I wanted to become. Of course, it being a cannabis event, I was high at that point. In response to him, as if it was the most natural thing in the world, I channeled an atemporal voice that flooded me in that moment:

"I am warrior,

I am Viking,

I will die when I am ready to die."

Once I blurted this mantra, I couldn't un-know it. It was like a rune tattooed in my soul long ago, now activated. I am a different person on the other side of this experience. I dove to the deepest depths and crossed oceans like a Viking. The warrior inside me is stronger and the inner child softer. They hold hands and laugh. The warrior will always be there to vanquish fear and protect little Alice with infinite love.

Songs to feel like a warrior:
Sia - Unstoppable
Beethoven - 5th Symphony
Eminem - Lose Yourself

About the Author
Alice Stark

Alice Stark is driven by a passion for crafting stories that inspire courage and instill a desire for a juster world. Alice's humble upbringing, her corporate trauma and her travels to forty countries inspired in her a profound respect for the diversity and resilience of the human spirit. Alice believes that we each have the seed of self-love within and we just have to water it. The Lawsuit story is meant to awaken the warrior seed within each of us. Often when we go through difficult situations we feel alone. I am here to remind you that you are not alone. Women warriors are going to be leading the evolution of humanity and I am here to remind you that there is a warrior inside each one of us that has to protect our innocence and that of the generations to come.

www.maincharacter.energy

IG: maincharacterenergy.me

Chapter Nine

I CAN AND I DO ... BUT NOT NOW
GLORIA COTTON

Here's the scenario: you have the skill, confidence, and reputation of being a good coach or analyst, a celebrated innovator and leader, etc. You're not a legend in your own mind. Others have told you and you've been rewarded for being a G.O.A.T. (Greatest Of All Time). And you've earned that rep because you've done the formal and informal work needed to excel. You've taken classes, earned certifications, completed courses of study, and secured degrees. You self-assess your strengths and needs and have been assessed and evaluated by others with all feedback pointing to your exceptional skills and ability to create relationships and a culture that are safe and inclusive. Self-reflection, self-examination and self-assessment are the norm for you. And you show up as a mentor, coach, role model, leader, manager, and ally for everyone. Safe to say, you rock—but not today. Why? Simple. You're human. And, let's face it, even rock stars like you don't shine brightly all the time. Have you had one of those days when you know you can give great feedback, but not now, not in this moment, this situation and circumstance? Have you ever had that experience? I know I have. In this chapter, we'll talk about some simple steps you can take to build trust and stronger teams when you're having one of those "not now" days.

One of my mental visuals of myself and others is that we are not onions who can simply peel back layers. Human beings are way more complex than an onion. It's not just that we have layers; we're like a bulb of garlic and each of our cloves is a different size, with a different amount of juiciness, and each clove has layers. Using this mindset, I was able to understand why it was that when I thought I had mastered something, had finally worked through an issue and found *the* answer, I could still find myself facing it again. Even though I had been there and done that, it was way back. But, even though it seemed like the same thing initially, the closer I looked to assess and understand, I noticed nuanced differences. So, I encourage you to show yourself some grace and kindness when you're having an "off day." It's another opportunity to learn more, to expand your comfort and knowledge zones. Just be sure you've made enough deposits in the emotional bank accounts of others (and for yourself) so that when you miss the mark or get something wrong—and you will—your relationships can grow through the test.

Here's what I've learned to do as I examine and befriend each hiccup, mess up, and disappointment so that, instead of beating myself up, I can see them as opportunities and even enjoy them.

So what are some S.M.A.R.T. things we can do? First of all, don't deny, stop, or try to push away your feelings or your thoughts. Instead, **acknowledge them**. And (this is huge) love them. Love every single clove and layer of them. Imagine seeing, hearing, and experiencing each feeling and thought without judgment, without even having judgments about your judgments, or allowing yourself to drown in the judgments of others. I literally meet each thought and ask, "What message of love do you have for me?" Then I listen and have a conversation with them. Your feelings and thoughts did not just come out of nowhere. Your life has created them and they are part of you. They exist because of the things you have experienced directly and indirectly in your life. Sometimes, when I am particularly off-center, I say, "My life has earned this feeling (or thought)." To deny those things, to discount or try to shut them out or down, or to try to eliminate them makes about as much sense as my cutting off a body part and expecting it to not make a difference and to pretend I'm not in pain or bleeding out.

Remember that every living thing that can think and imagine—that includes you and me—wants to be seen, heard, and understood. Think about how often we don't allow ourselves to see or hear and truly understand our own needs, challenges, and perspectives. Ignoring joy or pain doesn't make them go away; it just makes them push harder to be seen, heard, and understood. Even if we go into fight, flight, freeze, or fawn mode and the feelings may not be as obvious as they once were or could be, they're still there and—one way or another—will not be denied.

So, the first thing we have to do is to acknowledge our feelings and thoughts—to acknowledge our whole, authentic selves. When we are representing, considering, and taking care of everyone else and sacrificing ourselves all the time, we will hit a wall. And when we hit that wall, we just don't have the energy, strength, or wherewithal to champion others—even though we may be a champion of champions. We need to face the in-the-moment truth that **I am a champion and I do love championing others, but not now.**

KEEP THESE THINGS IN YOUR HEART AND MIND

Establish true intimacy with yourself. Record your acknowledged thoughts and feelings. I mean just talk it out. Most newer laptops have a feature where, if you open a blank Word document, you can dictate or speak your words and it will type what you say as you say it. Is it perfect? No. When I use it, I have to manually add punctuation, paragraphs, indentations, etc., as I'm editing it. But what's delicious is that I can just *be*. That is, I can speak freely without having to weigh what I'm saying or be concerned with syntax, grammar, or anything that might delay or give a different texture or flavor to my in-the-moment truth. What are some of the benefits of this approach?

- It's fast.
- I can actually read it. For instance, my handwriting is atrocious when I'm trying to write fast. And I definitely can't write or type as fast as I can speak. And sometimes I just need to regurgitate or "word vomit" about my thoughts and feelings.

- It's conversational and, therefore, more accessible and relatable.
- There's a joy in not censoring myself, in just letting things flow so that I feel totally free. This is particularly an oxygen-giver if I've felt stifled or felt that my voice was not welcome, heard, or understood. Writing using the dictation tool energizes me and that's why I love it. Keep in mind: if writing things out in longhand or typing them gives you that sense of exhilaration and freedom, by all means, do that. The thing is for you to connect with yourself where you may have felt disconnected from others or yourself before.
- You'll be able to hear and understand the "why." Why you feel and think as you do—what's behind those feelings and thoughts, the history, and the anticipated future?
- You get a bonus benefit when you go back to read what you've written aloud so that you hear and feel the vibration of those words—perhaps for the first time. As you edit and add more stuff, notice the increase in peace, clarity, calmness, excitement, and creativity that you feel in every drop of water in every drop of blood within your body. It's really delicious. So I encourage you, do not read it silently. Read aloud as if you're sharing what you've written with someone special because you *are.* You're sharing it with you.

Next, *validate your feelings and thoughts.* People often talk about how we "get in our feelings." I'm here to tell you that we get into our judgments just as often and sometimes more quickly. Not only do we judge others, we judge ourselves. And sometimes we're merciless. Is it any wonder we're exhausted? Without being consciously intentional, we may find ourselves operating from a fixed and closed mindset: exaggerating and fixating on the negative, minimizing the positive, and focusing on what we haven't done while ignoring what we have done. When I do that I sometimes feel like a hamster running on the wheel but getting nowhere fast. But sometimes I'm so cool that others see me as the duck gliding on water and giving the appearance that everything is okay when I'm really working hard to maintain. A huge miss when these things happen is that I may forget to ask for help or refuse the help of others when they offer it. Can you say burnout, martyrdom, and levels of fight, flight, freeze, or faint?

I love the book *Atomic Habits* by James Clear. One of my strongest takeaways from the pearls of wisdom Mr. Clear shares in that book is that we often set goals and may even identify milestones to achieve them. But (and here's the opportunity) we either don't celebrate the incremental milestones of the larger milestones, or the celebration is so quick and lackluster that we allow it to pass without any kind of meaningful acknowledgment. Now, pay attention to the word, "meaningful." We're a culture that values being busy, doing, producing, and executing. Have you ever counted up all the things you have done and then asked yourself, "So what?" Is it about quantity and being busy for the sake of being busy, or are we strategically busy so that our efforts are actually tied to the greatest needs and make the most positive impact and difference? Talk about hamster wheels and sailing ducks! Is it any wonder we sometimes have "...but not now" experiences?!

KEEP THESE THINGS IN YOUR HEART AND MIND

Validation is about looking at your feelings and thoughts without judgment and with ties to things that make a real difference, considering everyone's perspective and needs. When we don't validate and align our doing with the real needs, we begin to burn through all our fuel, our passion. And flying on empty, we're subject to crash and burn and create a "... not now" experience. So instead:

- Validate, embrace and celebrate big and small things that make a meaningful, positive difference to someone, somewhere, somehow.
- Ask and answer the "why" questions, not just the what, when, how much, where and who questions.
- Identify qualitative as well as quantitative measures of success.

- Look at everything as an opportunity to learn or confirm that your doing is aligned with your personal as well as professional mission/purpose.

And, finally, **give yourself permission** to change your path or direction, to reboot, reinvent and renew so that your heart sings, your mind dances and your soul soars.

First, discover, claim and bask in your answer or answers to those things. Many times as I am serving people as a life coach, they won't have a clue how to answer those things. They know about obligation, responsibility, accountability and what others expect of them. And most of the time they're good at and are well-prepared for them as they live their lives for someone else's happiness while sacrificing their own or operating from old patterns and habits that used to serve but no longer do. Many times they enjoy or at least content themselves with doing those things. But there can be a level of resignation that is fueled by a lack of the excitement and innocence they once experienced in their youth. Some people seem to expect that as they get older, they will play and enjoy living less. I think that's interesting and find that I actively seek and ask about "fun" in almost everything I do. I ask, "Are you having fun?" And I surely ask, "Glo, are you having fun?" And, if not, why not? Can you bring the joie de vivre into what you're doing or change what you're doing (what, how, how long, with whom, when, where, etc.)? Either way, I encourage you to find your joy – inside and outside.

I remember telling a woman who was feeling overwhelmed with what she had to do within a certain period, and she was definitely not celebrating milestone accomplishments. I listened without judgment and supported her by giving her the space and time she needed to state her fears and frustrations and acknowledging and validating her, what she said and her experience. When she stopped, our conversation went like this:

Me: Are you finished? Is there more you need or would like to add?

She: No. Nothing more. I'm just overwhelmed.

Me: Queen, you've got to get in touch with your royalty.

She: What?

Me: You've got to get in touch with your royalty. Can you tell me three things you've done just today that have not only met your goals but have helped people in ways they weren't expecting?

I know this woman. And I know that on a slow day, she is doing things that make a noticeable difference in people's lives, not only meeting but exceeding their expectations while all the while building their trust and confidence in themselves. Isn't it interesting how we sometimes undervalue our value?

Me: Now, please look at that list of things you said you had to do and hadn't made a dent in. How do you see those things now?

She: I've actually done some of them! I've delegated some others and just hadn't taken them off my to-do list. I can breathe again. Thank you! You know what, I just need to speak with you every day, Glo.

Me: I'm here for you.

It's definitely time to ask yourself, "If not now, when?"

KEEP THESE THINGS IN YOUR HEART AND MIND

- Give yourself permission to be the uncompromisingly awesome person that you are
- Set goals and milestones and C-E-L-E-B-R-A-T-E good times, come on!! (Shout out to Kool & The Gang! Thanks for the song, Celebration!)
- Align your doing (accomplishments and deliverables) with your being (who and what you are)
- Remember that you deserve to be and do things that:

  Make your heart sing like a choir of your favorite music-makers
  Make your mind dance with the discovery of discovery and learning and applying
  Make your soul soar with unlimited and undefined possibilities

About the Author
Gloria Cotton

Gloria Cotton is an author and Leadership Optimization Consultant, speaker, coach and facilitator. She helps people fall in love with themselves for the first time or again so they can be more authentic and optimally successful at home, at work and in their communities by helping them understand and apply pragmatic models and processes and real-world how-to tips.

She is a contributing author in By The Light of the Moon. On her podcast, The Delicious Truth Podcast with Gloria Cotton, she interviews business and community leaders about issues that impact our daily lives and how to discuss them in ways that build awareness and trust when those conversations are easy or challenging.

Having worked with global organizations, "Glo" is respected and sought after for helping people create environments and relationships where everyone can be and do their best. A native of Chicago, "Glo" now lives in Elgin, Illinois.

Chapter Ten

A TOWER MOMENT
ALE KANASHIRO

A s I walked into the doctor's office with my sister, we were finally going to become US residents, which we had waited for over 10 years to become. We sit there in the doctor's office to get the required check-up to become residents, and we get a call that we need to go to the Emergency Room because my sister's platelets were dangerously low. Platelets? What is that even?

We rush through and find out that my sister has cancer... boom. The world felt like it had caved in on my family and me.

Stage 4 they said.

Boom.

What? Why? How? Does something greater even exist? What is the purpose of this?

Tower moments. The words echoed in my mind like a mantra in a loop. Tower moments shake you, they rattle you to your core. You wonder, trying to grasp any logic as to WHY this is happening. Did you do something to deserve this? How will I find the strength to get through this? Can I even get through this? What should I do? While you are in them it feels so foggy, so messy, it makes you question *everything*.

These moments strip away the layers of comfort, forcing us to confront our deepest fears and vulnerabilities. They are so crucial for our experience to align our paths again, and to offer a perspective shift. While they might leave us with some scars and a bit bruised, they show us just how capable we are and how we can create change within.

As much as we want to avoid these moments or even the moments when we feel at a total loss, we get to embrace them. Squeeze the lessons, sink deeper with ourselves, and transform through it to the other side, and *become*.

As we maneuvered what felt like a whole new territory of the *cancer* world, we leaned into it. My sister was the bravest person I have ever met and she embraced this new challenge as an adventure. She would take advantage of all of the activities the hospital had to offer. We would leave each chemotherapy session with a new craft, a new skill, or with our eyes hurting from the amount of video games we battled in those hours. We went to every event they offered, like swimming with dolphins, going to a cancer prom, and riding on private yachts.

We went to more concerts than we would ever have before, we savored each moment and made the absolute best thing out of it. We cherished our life and didn't take it for granted. Living life before that felt like we were robots in human form.

A whole new level of living was *unlocked*.

Every tower moment that my clients and I have ever gone through has helped us unlock the next level of life. A new level of trust. As a hypnotherapist and a transformational coach, I work with my clients to navigate difficult times, change coping mechanisms, and transform themselves inside and out. We work through belief systems that are not serving them, on healing parts of themselves that are holding them back, and creating a transformation that truly lasts.

As humans, we like to stay comfortable and we might need a rude awakening. Even though it's painful, it is exactly what we need. Taking a look at what area of your life the tower moment is happening to can help you get clarity on what needs some attention.

I am not saying my sister deserved to have cancer, but her cancer opened us up to a way of living we can never turn back on. It changed our whole perspective on life, health, what it means to be human on this earth, and how often we take it for granted.

Tower moments can look very different for each person.

Tower moments can feel different for each person.

But they always have a purpose, a realigning element to them.

Embrace them and allow the transformation to take place.

For example, if you are having a tower moment in the area or finances, it would be beneficial to take a look at what was not in alignment. Is there something you need to learn about? Be more conscious about? What lessons is this moment giving you that you can integrate into life?

If it was in the area of love, what is this teaching you need or want in a relationship? Is there something you need to integrate to have better relationships? Any wounds that need to be addressed? What are your nonnegotiables in relationships?

Remember that since we are humans and we love our comfort zone, sometimes the only way to get us to change is when drastic things happen so there is no other way than change.

When I hit one of my biggest financial rock bottoms, it taught me that I was worth more than just how much money I made. No matter how much money I chased, it would never feel enough. I chased $10K a month, hit that, and still felt like I needed more. I chased until I burned out, all to show me that it's not about the number in my bank account, that my value is not dependent on how much money I make or what status I have in the world. I also took a deeper look at where I need to set some boundaries around money, where I need to be more conscious of it, and how I can start to invest it properly. When I transcended that and integrated that lesson, everything started to flow again. Sometimes you get things taken away from you to realize that you can survive without it, that your value goes beyond that.

Tower moments are not permanent and they take less time when we integrate the lessons and trust.

The problem with many tower moments is that we don't trust them. We don't surrender to them, we tighten. We don't want to let go of the grip. And when we lose the resistance, we sink into the process and become aware. You will start to see everything unfold, just how it needs to. We trust that our path needs alignment. We trust that, for things to find their way, we need things to get reorganized or some things to fall away.

SO HOW DO WE IDENTIFY TOWER MOMENTS IN OUR LIVES?

This usually involves events in your life where your comfort zone is being ripped away. This can be a relationship that you weren't fully happy in or wasn't in full alignment. This can be a sudden career transition where you lose a job you've had but you haven't been wanting to let go because you have been scared to do so. It can be misaligned friendships leaving your life that you were having a hard time letting go of. Sudden health scares that can feel like everything is caving in around you.

When you look closer into these events, you can see where the misalignment was. Where you truly needed to let go of something or some people and you needed a little intervention or you needed to learn a lesson to grasp this area of your life better.

The relationship ending that hurt letting go of in many ways was paving the way for a more aligned partnership. You get to see what you love about the relationship and what are things you've learned about yourself in relationships that you know you need in the ones moving forward. This type of awareness creates a door to your next level. It helps you create consciously based on the experiences that you have had.

Getting fired from a job that you knew was no longer bringing you fulfillment can leave you feeling worried when you make this about yourself. When you make this single event define your worth rather than a moment to learn from. What could you have done better? What do you desire in your next position? What would feel even bigger than this?

This can be applied to all areas of life and with any tower moment.

As we've talked about, tower moments come with a lot of letting go.

They can often involve a process of grieving because they require letting go of certain aspects of your life. This could include relationships, jobs, beliefs, habits, or identities that are no longer serving you or aligning with your true self. This can cause you to miss what you once had, be scared of the unknown, and confront many different emotions that will arise from letting things go.

So when you are going through these moments, hold yourself through the emotions you are feeling. They are all valid and a part of the human experience, knowing that when you allow emotions to be there, they move through way quicker than you'd think. Regardless of how long it takes, being present with your emotions is the best way to go through grief.

As your old identities, relationships, or careers settle in the past, you have a new opportunity to rebuild with much more knowledge this time. Use this for your benefit. You are turning a brand new page in your book. You have a fresh new start and so much space from what has fallen apart. Utilize it to find alignment and create the life you know you are meant to have. Let the catastrophes connect you deeper with your emotions and feelings. Allow these tower moments to increase your capacity to hold this human experience, to show you how resilient you truly are, and how you can take the mess and create magic. We all can and sometimes it takes moments like these to show you just how much you can truly hold and transcend.

As for my sister, while she battled 2 rounds of cancer, we traveled around the United States and she traveled to Morocco, Spain, Lisbon, and Peru. We would go for her chemotherapy appointment and ask about how traveling could fit into this. She was an avid traveler. She was determined that cancer wasn't going to take over her life. She wasn't cancer, she was a human with a life that had cancer. We tried many things, we tried holistic practices, we went to church.

After 6 months of remission, we finally celebrated my graduation from high school. Everyone was gathered and we went to our graduation and went to eat at the steakhouse we love. We had planned a trip to Peru where we were FINALLY going to go to Machu Picchu a day after my orientation for college since I was starting in the summer semester. Everyone was so happy and enjoying the unlimited meat that was going around, but there was something off. My sister barely touched her food and that was VERY unlike her. My sister is a total carnivore. So we all thought that she was just not as hungry.

We went home and the next day my sister called me into her room. She grabs my hand and places it on the side of her throat and my eyes widen. I know what this is... memories flood back, terror fills every fiber of my body, and my eyes fill up. This can't be happening *again. Boom.*

This can't be happening again.

We get an appointment to get it checked and they tell us it's back. They tell us that they don't recommend that we go on the trip. We had to cancel everything. We had to get into treatment again. We had to do it *again*. How much strength is enough strength?

I started college. Blurry. I would drive to and from the hospital, blurry. One day, I get to the hospital and we're having a meeting. This meeting was different than most: it was with the social worker, the doctor, my dad, and my uncle. We sit in this room and you can feel it. You can feel that something is coming and you don't even know what it is, but your body knows, your body feels.

The social worker translates things into Spanish for my dad and uncle to understand. Terminal is what I picked up as soon as it left her mouth. Terminal. *Boom. except this boom, truly shook EVERYTHING so silently.*

My dad couldn't wrap his head around it, my uncle sat there like he was completely disassociated, and I... I couldn't feel my body. I wanted to curl up in a fetal position. Where was the escape button? Where was the I didn't choose this life, can I exchange it?

We walked back to the room where my sister and my mom were and I just lay in that bed with her. I don't even fully remember if we said anything, blurry.

My dad pleaded that we find another solution. I can't imagine how helpless you must feel to not be able to do anything. My dad brought up a treatment they did in Mexico that had a good success rate. He wasn't giving up without a fight. My sister sat there and with a courage that I don't even know where it came from, she respectfully declined. She was tired, she was finished.

For what? Quality over quantity.
Boom.

Truly tuning into knowing when to let go.

Each person in my family maneuvered through this differently. We come from an Asian background where feelings and emotions are not felt or even more so talked about.

For me, it completely changed my view on life, and on our purpose on this earth. I see death and life very differently than most, I don't fear it. I see it like a video game. My sister had finished this level. She had completed her journey here, she had done all of her quests, gained all of the skills, and impacted all the people she needed to impact. She had *leveled up.*

Why would she keep repeating this level?

Why would she not go to the next level? Because of us? No.

I truly believe we all come to this life for a reason. There is a purpose for us. It doesn't have to be this huge purpose like most people think or make it out to be. Sometimes the most important purpose is the close people you impact.

Sometimes, your passing will be your biggest purpose. It will create change for so many people it's crazy.

Your presence creates ripple effects. When you impact those around you, they impact those around them, and the world slowly but surely becomes a better place.

My sister impacted more people than I think she knew. She fought until the end and did it so gracefully it was criminal.

So while tower moments can be so hard, can feel like everything is falling apart, sink into them, and be there with them. There are nuggets. They are part of your life journey, of your human experience. I invite you to embrace it fully and integrate.

About the Author
Ale Kanashiro

I'm a hypnotherapist and a transformational mentor. Working deeply with the subconscious mind, healing your inner child wounds, and creating safety within you has unlocked everything for myself and so many of my clients.

I guide you to discover deeply who you are by integrating your shadow aspects, gaining a good understanding of what an aligned life looks like for you, healing the trauma that has you stuck with unwanted coping mechanisms, and creating safety in taking action toward your alignment.

bit.ly/AK-Workwithme

Chapter Eleven

SPAWNED

NATHALIA MARIN

No one invited me into freedom, not ever. I had to walk myself to that physical and spiritual place where beautiful things manifest, and where the only way to get in is by letting go, repeatedly, incessantly.

I wanted to be free.

I prayed for it.

Begged and cried for it.

The pain entangled me, owned me. It was the only thing I could think of and desired for years.

I caught myself dreaming of being someone else, being somewhere else, and having the strength to exhale all the pain. But it had always been within me; I was the pain, and the bravest thing I could do was to die.

My life as I remember it has always been complicated. I was very loved, but not in the way I needed. I can't blame anyone for this. I am happy I was born, but the process of becoming who I am today was long and painful.

There is nothing more painful than seeing yourself and not accepting absolutely anything about it, and because of that, all my decisions led me to the same deep hole of not wanting to be me, or wanting to be someone else—someone with a dad, with a mom, with her own room to be safe in. And someone who did not have to be enough for anyone else, just me.

How many times will I need to let go of what is heavy? How many times will I have to start over and re-teach myself that I am the safest place in the entire world?

But let's go back a little. I was born in Medellin, Colombia at a time of great political uncertainty. Colombia was known for drug trafficking.

My mom was seventeen when I was born. I remember having a friend more than having a mother. Smoking together, partying together, hangovers. She ignored the red flags of this toxic relationship, and I blamed her. I find myself now owning this pain like never before, but also wondering what it would have been like if she had taken care of my needs, what it would have been like to be seen.

I always wondered what she was like at 17, how much life was hurting for her at that moment. And then I showed up. Grandma was my primary caretaker until she left the country when I was three years old. She was chasing the American Dream, at 34 years old—a widow, with four kids, and one grandchild. Life also had to hurt deeply for her. I was instantly unattended when she left the country, and 1985 was the beginning of it all. All my troubles began when Grandma departed.

By the time she was 24, my mother and I had moved at least eight times until we settled with a man and his family for a while. A couple of years later my mother had another daughter. My sister, Baby, as I call her to this day. She was such a joy in my life, but also a burden to our 24-year-old mother, who was once again a single mother (things didn't work out with the man).

No job, no home, but an empty house, some mattresses, a big cassette player, and the promise of American dollars every other week sent by Grandma. Also...more men.

Consistently inconsistent pretend father figures came in and out to love her a little and then left until one day Juan came. Proud of his good looks, tall and skinny, permanent smile, dark skin, and no hair, Juan stayed a bit longer. He stayed long enough for me to remember him today.

Juan taught me good music. We would listen to Chicago and the Police, all of this while not drinking alcohol. He was perfect. He taught me how to be happy and simple. He was happy regardless of the circumstances. He would dance to "Your Love" by The Outfield and laugh. I enjoyed his presence and his free spirit; he also respected and enjoyed mine, and he seemed to see eye-to-eye with me. A difficult job for the rest of the world, but it was easy for Juan.

My mom's relationship with Juan wasn't functional in the slightest, but he and I got along better than I did with my mom. Time flew by, I grew up to understand that the world around me was not emotionally safe. Meanwhile, the Colombian drug problems grew. In the 80s, Pablo Escobar became the drug lord everyone knows about—the king and ruler of Medellin, and the entire world.

I was introduced to cocaine at the age of 10. By 12, I was rolling and smoking any type of plant that crossed my path, especially marijuana. We were living in one of the most dangerous neighborhoods in Medellin, Barrio Nuevo, small with no police presence even when shootings were the daily bread. My friends taught me everything I needed to know about drug dealing, and surviving, basically on my own. My friends became my safe place. Cristina was a couple of years older than me. She was the bravest, and meanest girl I knew. But to me she was sweet and loving. She was my protector. In exchange, I was her provider of novelty, international candy, and international shoes. She loved all the new tennis shoes my grandma sent me from the States. She kept them sparkling clean. In the neighborhood, she fought girls who called me names. Cristina became my big sister.

I played hide and seek a couple of times before I was delivering bullets around the neighborhood from house to house, with fear, but with no choice and always in secrecy. I pretended to be a "normal" kid. I loved to play outside and dance in the rain whenever I had a chance. But the reality was different.

My father promised he would come but he never did. He sent some money, a sweater, and a key chain. I burned it all in my consuming pain; I watched it burn. I blamed him for leaving me behind.

Escobar was killed in 1993, and so were all my friends. After my mother received an anonymous call saying I was going to be the next to die, we ran away to the United States: without clothes, without permission, without saying goodbye. We just ran in a real hurry. A bus took us to Ecuador with only one bag on my back. Forged papers allowed us to flee; 48 hours later we met Grandma at Newark Airport.

I wasn't the same. Grandma wasn't the same. Nothing was the same, and it never would be. Our relationship had space in it. Since she has been in my life, I have had so many grandmas and so many moms. In her absence, neighbors and friends had taken me under their wings. Cristina and Juan's mother fed us and opened their doors for us in the most difficult times of our lives.

Now in the USA, our room at Grandma's house was small. The closet doors were covered in mirrors; it made it look bigger, but it was just an illusion. The green carpet reminded me how limited my space was. Our two windows were thick, like nothing I had seen before. I needed to sustain my secret smoking habit. No one knew about it; no one knew about me at all.

"Why are the windows so thick?"

"The windows will keep you warm during the winter," Grandma said.

"Can they be opened?" I asked.

"Of course." She showed me how and walked out of the room.

I got my cigarette and lighter and blew the smoke out the screened window. No one noticed– it was their specialty.

In this new place, I started collecting memories, places, and smells. I still like them all.

The smell of gas as the stove was turned on when cooking. The smell of a house, so unknown to me, a house with functional furniture, and a chimney, like in the movies. Laundry detergent and shampoo were luxuries that I could get used to, and I did. Grandma was affluent, and I soon learned that. She would shower me with gifts: VHS movies, clothing, and shoes that I wished I could send Cristina. But I had lost contact with her after we left.

If it wasn't traumatic enough to be in another country, my mom started working 12-hour shifts so I spent most of my time in school or with Grandma and Baby. Slowly, I changed. I started dressing differently, doing my nails and my hair differently. My heart was different. I finally felt like I belonged again. But just when I was feeling rooted, my mother decided to move to Florida. Florida was sunny and pretty, but I was separated from Grandma again.

Everything went downhill from there. Grandma was not there to care for me anymore. No one was. Cristina was killed a few days after I arrived in Florida. I didn't know how to feel, so I didn't. I preferred to be numb: parties and drugs and silence. I granted myself all escape; no one was to come in between me and my pain. The pain of living was too big for me. It was evident by all my destructive behavior: drug consumption, eating disorders, drunk driving, unprotected sex, occasional fainting, panic attacks, prescribed Xanax, and Xanax dependency. All I wanted was to be free from feeling.

No one invited me to freedom. The freedom I so desperately craved was not near, and no one seemed to possess it. It was unknown, nonexistent. Freedom was a mystery. It seemed to be available to only some chosen ones, but not to me.

Financial freedom was the most prominent freedom I craved and envied the most. It became my goal to acquire some of that freedom, but all my efforts seemed in vain. Unless I gave some of my soul or my body away, money was not befriending me. When did I decide to abandon my soul? I'm not certain. But I did, as many times as needed. I became an expert at letting go of myself completely. Let go, start over, let go, start over.

I learned to let go for months, years, decades, until one day I noticed myself, noticed the pain.

Letting go of something you are and recreating yourself seems easy in theory, but the transition will leave you feeling lost, confused, angry, invisible, and empty. The separation between who you are and who you are becoming is painful. But I had to choose which pain to endure.

FREEDOM GROWS HERE

During a hot summer day in Florida, taking my first psychology class as an elective course, I fell deeply in love. For a moment I got a hint about the complexity of the human mind. I saw my mind, and I was blown away. I decided I wanted to dive into the human mind. I needed to understand my mind. It has been 19 years since that day, and I have gathered an indescribable amount of knowledge about the human mind.

I discovered beautiful tools and techniques. I took this journey myself. And now I can share with others the magical world of self-compassion and self-acceptance, the opposite of self-abandonment. I can navigate the pain of others and guide them to the most beautiful places where freedom grows.

Self-abandonment is not something we choose consciously. We are taught by people who offer no other choice because they know no other way. No one has children intending to hurt or destroy them. But it is our responsibility to hope for a better understanding of our pain. To offer self-compassion in a world full of guilt is revolutionary. Nonetheless, it is difficult. Our brains are designed to see the worst, to identify the pain. Compassion and radical acceptance are not natural to traumatized minds. We need training. Even the simple option of choosing a different thought can change the course of one's life.

I chose to move. I didn't have to stay in the same place. I permitted myself to be a different person. I chose differently. This time I was given the option. I gave myself the option because no one was coming to rescue me, I did it for myself. I have been fortunate, I believe. My pain has been my greatest teacher.

Understanding pain is one thing; loving it is a journey in itself. The idea of loving myself was new. The journey to a new life was great. I finally didn't have to erase the pain that had haunted me. The beauty behind the pain has been bigger.

The promise of another way of being was not something I could physically hold on to, like a flower in my hand. It was more like an idea, a thought, like a smell, or the memory of a voice.

I needed to hold on tight to that idea, until it became real, until it was mine forever. It took time, almost two decades, to become the love of my life. It has been subtle, and revolutionary; it has been life-changing but never easy.

The amount of consistent forgiveness and letting go has been enormous: letting go of the pain I was holding on to for years, the pain I was born into was the most comfortable place to be, the only one I knew.

Everything we know about ourselves we keep in our soul, even our favorite color is stored there.

The soul of a human being is considered the intangible part that lives in the body and gives us the ability to think and feel, is the immaterial essence that defines us. All our things are stored there, from our favorite food to our childhood memories. The body is one of our most important aspects. But without our souls, we are nothing. So why do we usually invest the least in it? I had abandoned my soul, maybe we all have at some point in our lives. I didn't know any better.

The abandonment was unintentional; no one abandons something they need deliberately.

Our soul is as important and fundamental as our body. Without a body, we simply cannot function on this planet. The same thing happens with the soul; illness in the mind also limits us. For generations, humans have learned to live with these limitations, or with the abandonment of the soul, but when we heal we have many more opportunities to reach our potential. When we heal our body and our mind there is no turning back. With the awakening of the soul, we can find our purpose and our freedom: physical, emotional, financial, and in every area of our life. It is a wonderful thing. It's a manifestation of the spirit here on earth, almost indescribable.

The most challenging task lies in acknowledging your own reality. The lonely nights, the lonely roads, the denial, the anger, the hope, and the despair. To open your mind wide enough to confront your brokenness and the feelings of scarcity is a daunting journey. I had to navigate the dark recesses of my soul, confronting and comprehending them before finally embracing them. Taking ownership of your narrative marks the beginning of the healing process, even if no one else acknowledges it or agrees. Your story is genuine, and you have every right to perceive it.

In finding freedom, I liberated not only myself but also my two sons and future generations. This freedom, which I yearned for so intensely, was ultimately mine. The healing belongs to me, as does the process itself. In the dying and the spawning, here I am.

I am free.

About the Author
Nathalia Marin

Nathalia was born in Medellin, Colombia. She moved to the United States at a young age where she completed her studies in psychology. Nathalia moved back to Colombia after 25 years, and now works as a therapist and specializes in helping adults identify and change their lifestyle. She is a strong believer in the essence of human beings often shadowed by personality. The core of her practice is to uncover the essence and find our purpose.

She is a speaker, writer, and teacher. Her hobbies include painting, reading, and skating, most of the time with her two boys and husband.

You can book a session with her, or visit her blog where she writes weekly in Spanish with an option to translate to English.

linktr.ee/nathaliamarin

Thank you

Dear Reader,

If you have enjoyed or found value in this book, please take a moment to leave an honest/brief review on Amazon amzn.to/4d9luo5 or Goodreads. Your reviews help prospective readers decide if this is right for them & it is the greatest kindness you can offer the authors.

Thank you in advance.

Acknowledgments

This book is the result of countless moments from mentors, teacher and guides. It is the culmination of our our dreams and the learning from our own struggles. It is in this process of writing that we both share our vulnerable selves and offer a gift forth for the readers.

In particular our author mentors that supported writers:

- Frances D. Trejo-Lay
- Jessical Goldmutz Stokes
- Erika Hull

These women have shared, coached and guided the contributors through technical, logistical and emotional journey that is writing and becoming an author.

Thanks to all who have led us to this moment. May it ripple.

Other Red Thread Books

OUR BOOKS ABOUT WRITING & PUBLISHING:

The Anatomy of a Book: 21 Book Experts Share What Aspiring Authors Need to Know About Writing, Publishing & Book Marketing

Typo: The Art of Imperfect Creation, *Permission to Do it Badly*

Story Ink: *A Cyclical Methodology to Write 1 or 100 books* (2024)

Write: *An Interactive Guide to Drafting Your Manuscript* (forthcoming)

To see all our published works Visit Our Library:

bit.ly/RedThreadLibrary

PREVIOUS COLLABORATIVE TITLES IN THE BRAVE NEW VOICES SERIES:

Feisty: *Dangerously Amazing Women Using Their Voices & Making An Impact*

Spark: *Women in the Business of Changing the World*

Sanctuary: *Cultivating Safe Space in Sisterhood; Rediscovering the Power that Unites Us*

Planting the Seed: *Lessons to Cultivate a Brighter Future*

Notes From Motherland: *The Wild Adventure of Raising Humans*

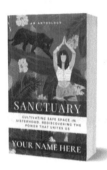

Sisterhood Redefines Us (Collaborative)

We are stronger together, but we must find or create our own safety first. (10 authors)

Dangerously Amazing Women (Collaborative)

If you're ready to rewrite all the rules & start thriving, just as you are, then Feisty is a must-read! (19 authors)

Women In the Business of Changing the World (Collaborative)

Celebrating the extraordinary impact of ordinary women, women when we show up & shine in our full, unapologetic authority. (10 authors)

WRITE & PUBLISH WITH US AS A COLLABORATIVE AUTHOR

Be the next **Red Thread Collaborative Author**: bit.ly/46Yd6Ed

Why write with us

Our collaborative authors get full support in the drafting, editing and publishing process. We teach all our authors about book marketing & authorprenur essentials. We work as a collective and have a wider reach and more impact as a result.

If a book is like a baby, writing in a collaborative is like being an auntie; all the joy with a fraction of the effort of writing and publishing an entire book yourself.

*All royalties from this book fund our Author Scholarship Program. We believe in powerful stories and support otherwise silenced voices to be heard.

≈

Access our Free Author Resources
bit.ly/RedThreadResources

Red Thread Publishing

Red Thread Publishing is an all-female publishing company on a mission to support 10,000 women to become successful published authorpreneurs & thought leaders.

To work with us or connect regarding any of our growing library of books email us at **info@redthreadbooks.com.**

To learn more about us visit our website **www.redthreadbooks.com.**

Follow us & join the community.

facebook.com/redthreadpublishing

instagram.com/redthreadbooks

Made in United States
Troutdale, OR
06/04/2024

20319677R00076